"I loved it. I wish I had written this book myself."
**Richard Dreyfuss**

"Anybody who loves Hollywood movies should read this book."
**Robert Altman**

"A fascinating peek into the making of one of Hollywood's best movies."
**Susan Sarandon**

"A fascinating peek into the making of the movie that
re-defined mashed potatoes."
**Tim Robbins**

"What all books about movies should be — a gem of insiderdom."
**Dick Cavett**

"A Close Encounter of the witty and informative kind."
**Richard E. Grant**

"Charmingly honest and endlessly enjoyable. ****"
*Empire*

to Grossman, the brightest and the best

# SPIELBERG, TRUFFAUT & ME

**SPIELBERG, TRUFFAUT & ME**
**CLOSE ENCOUNTERS OF THE THIRD KIND**
**AN ACTOR'S DIARY**
1 84023 430 X

Published by
Titan Books
A division of
Titan Publishing Group Ltd
144 Southwark St
London
SE1 0UP

First edition July 2002
10 9 8 7 6 5 4 3 2 1

**Acknowledgements**
Thanks to the following, without whose help this book wouldn't have been possible:
Tamara Rawitt; Marvin Levy; Steven Spielberg; Richard Dreyfuss; Melinda Dillon; Teri
Garr; Lucinda Valles; Mariah Taggart Balaban; Michael Kahn; Joe Alves; Dr. J. Allen Hynek;
Susan Heldfond; Clark Paylow; Larry Mark; Michael Singer; Gillian Marshall; Rawn
Harding; Maureen Davis; Sharon Charles; Sallie Charles; Lynn Darr; Mary Hendriques;
Marianne McGoldrick; Tamara Zurakowski. And Lynn Merrie Grossman.

Did you enjoy this book? We love to hear from our readers. Please e-mail us at:
**readerfeedback@titanemail.com** or write to Reader Feedback at the above address.

Titan Books' film and TV range are available from all good bookshops or direct from our mail
order service. For a free catalogue or to order, phone **01536 764646** with your credit card
details, or write to **Titan Books Mail Order, ASM Ltd, Unit 6, Pipewell Industrial Estate,
Desborough, Northants, NN14 2SW**. Please quote reference CE/3K.

To subscribe to our regular newsletter for up-to-the-minute news, great offers and competi-
tions, email: **titan-news@titanemail.com**

A CIP catalogue record for this title is available from the British Library.

Printed and bound in Great Britain by MPG, Bodmin, Cornwall.

Close Encounters
Of The Third Kind
An Actor's Diary

# SPIELBERG, TRUFFAUT & ME

BOB BALABAN

Introduction by
STEVEN SPIELBERG

TITAN BOOKS

# CONTENTS

# PREFACE

Twenty-five years ago I sat down to meet with Steven Spielberg, Richard Dreyfuss and Julia Phillips, and ended up spending six months working on a movie that changed my life. *Close Encounters of the Third Kind* opened to rave reviews and endless lines at the box office. I quickly transformed a stack of notes I had taken during filming into the book you're about to read. We sold out our first printing quickly. If you bought the book then, I hope you saved your copy, because I ran out and tried to buy one at a used book-store a couple of years ago, and it cost me seventy-five dollars. I never dreamed I'd become worthy of a sale on eBay.

In honor of the twenty-fifth anniversary of the movie, Titan is publishing this new, expanded version of my *Close Encounters of the Third Kind* diary with more pictures, and an additonal chapter looking back at the last two decades. Hope you have as much fun reading it as I had living it.

**Bob Balaban**
**Los Angeles, January 2002**

# INTRODUCTION

A word about Bob Balaban would be something like a report card home: "Dear Mr. and Mrs. Balaban: Robert is a quiet and well-behaved young man. He never speaks out of turn, and is always the first to raise his hand with the correct answer. His reassuring smile makes all those around him more agreeable. He often remains after class to straighten chairs. You must be very proud."

Having recently worked with Bob, it is my opinion that straightening chairs isn't exactly what Bob did after school. Perhaps Hamlet's "Poor Yorick..." soliloquy, or the 'Sempre Libera' aria from *Traviata* would be more like it. Or maybe Brando's tortured confession to Steiger from *On the Waterfront*, all performed to that empty classroom filled with crooked seats. That was my impression of Bob.

During the production of *Close Encounters*, many personal and often amusing incidents which were occurring every day would shoot right past me. The eye of a motion picture is not like the calm eye of a hurricane. This director remembers nothing but the pain, while others around me were having themselves a pretty good time.

I realized none of this until Bob sent me the manuscript of something he had been working on. This quiet and well-behaved actor who had always been so agreeable in the classroom, was busy keeping a journal after shooting each day! Bob Balaban's often hilarious observations showed me that no matter what the circumstances, no matter that a squall is blowing the set down, no matter that the extraterrestrials are on strike today, no matter that the bankers from New York are hollering, "How much is enough?" the humor of the life behind the scenes goes on and on and on.

I was concerned about what backstage life would be for Truffaut. He was, in fact, alone, a stranger in a very strange land. I felt that Bob was keeping François happy. He made him feel welcome. That was a responsibility that I also shared, but that he did better than I. François had a friend, somebody in the arid wilderness of Wyoming and Alabama whom he could speak with in his native tongue. I sometimes thought of Bob as François' daycare center.

I noticed François not being able to keep a smile off his face in one scene. I don't know why he was smiling. I thought it was some private observation François was making that I was supposed to see through the camera. I didn't realize that Bob and he had been telling each other jokes moments before the take. It was very confusing, because when I went to see the dailies, I kept searching the scenery for the source of François' amusement. The source of his amusement was standing right next to him with a beard and glasses.

Everybody on a film has a story to tell, and Bob Balaban's tale reassured me that as I was slowly losing my head, all those around me were also losing theirs.

**Steven Spielberg**

# FOREWORD

During 1976 and 1977, I spent six months of my life acting in a movie that promises to be one of the most successful films in movie history, *Close Encounters of the Third Kind*. I travelled with the movie to Wyoming; Mobile, Alabama; Bombay, India; the Mojave Desert and Hollywood. I worked and lived with a group of interesting and talented people that included two of the most gifted filmmakers of all time.

I kept a diary during this time, the *Close Encounters Diary*. Since all journalists and writers were barred during the shooting of the movie, my diary is the only on-the-spot account of the making of the movie, and the off-screen lives of the people involved in this enormous project.

Few of us (if any) realized that *Close Encounters* would turn out to be the block-buster movie it has become. For most of us *Close Encounters* was showing up for months at a time in hundred-degree-plus heat, pretending to see flying objects that weren't really there, and trying to lead as normal a life as possible in between. It wasn't easy; perhaps it never is.

Few books have chronicled the making of a major motion picture from the point of view of an actor. Acting in a movie, especially one with the scope of *Close Encounters*, can be a difficult experience. You spend very little of your time doing what you are actually hired to do — act. Mostly you wait, and you try to make the waiting as enjoyable as possible.

The waiting during *Close Encounters* was very enjoyable. Steven Spielberg, by his judicious hiring of actors and crew, and by the force of his personality created an atmosphere that was relaxed and happy; I was surrounded by interesting and friendly people who made what could have been a nightmare, a wonderful work experience.

My diary (as all diaries) is a subjective compilation of experiences and events. Since the film wasn't shot in sequence, the order in which scenes are described has nothing to do with the order in which they appear in the film. If this seems confusing, it *was* confusing. That confusion is part of the experience of being an actor in a film.

Occasionally I refer to an actor by his character's name, so I've included a cast list at the back of the diary. I've also included a crew list, since on a movie as massively technical as *Close Encounters*, the crew is an especially important and valued part of the movie making experience.

Some of the sequences never made it to the final print of the movie, and I've put an asterisk (*) after everything that was cut from the film.

I hope my diary gives you some idea of the real, non-glamorous, day-to-day process of the work of making a movie. In retrospect I have discovered that on *Close Encounters*, as in most movies, often the whole is greater than the sum of its parts.

**Bob Balaban**
**New York, February 1978**

Truffaut and I on location in India.

This is not a picture of Richard Dreyfuss. It's me, in 1976.

# PRE-PRODUCTION

**WEDNESDAY, MARCH 24, 1976**

I'm meeting with Steven Spielberg today about a part in a movie called *Close Encounters of the Third Kind*. I asked if I could read a script and was told *nobody* gets to read the script; they're being very secretive about it.

Spielberg's in a conference room at Juliette Taylor's casting office. We talk about how nice it is to be finally meeting. He looks very young. Richard Dreyfuss, who'll star in the movie, is there, too. We say how nice it is to see each other again, and talk about old times. He looks very young. I'm introduced to Julia Phillips, the film's producer. She looks very young, too. We talk and joke and laugh together, and have a terrifically casual and relaxed time, and then it dawns on me that Columbia Pictures has just given these very young-looking people twelve million dollars to make a movie. Spielberg tells me about the film. It's about UFOs, he says, but it is not science fiction. He calls it "science fact". He's considering me for the part of a French interpreter.

He asks me to say a couple of words in French. I say, "Il y avait longtemps depuis que j'ai parlé français, et si vous me donnez ce rôle, je devrais beaucoup étudier. En effet, je ne sais pas si je pourrais le faire." I say this in very rapid French which I have been rehearsing all morning. Roughly translated, it means: "I haven't spoken French in years, and if you give me the job I don't know if I'll be able to do it." Spielberg is impressed. He doesn't speak French. He says I sound great, he likes my work, and I have the job. I don't know if I should be excited; it all seems very unreal.

Spielberg tells me I will work for twenty weeks. That sounds good. He also says that if they can get him, I will be doing all my scenes with François Truffaut. That sounds wonderful. He says we will be working in Alabama, Wyoming, India and... Outer Mongolia. That sounds silly; I almost laugh.

Spielberg thinks I look like Dreyfuss. Since Dreyfuss has shaved his beard for the movie, I must keep mine.

I'm in somewhat of a daze. I hurry home and look up India and Outer Mongolia in my atlas. They're very far away.


**MARCH 26**

My agent calls me. Columbia is actually starting negotiations for the movie. I don't believe it. It's real. All those hours of "je parle, tu parles, il parle," are finally paying off. I keep thinking about how proud Miss Bessant, my ninth grade French teacher, will be. (She wrote in my yearbook, "Doesn't speak French that well, but has a nice smile.")

I tell people the name of the movie and nobody can understand what I'm saying. I have to repeat the title very slowly, syllable by syllable: "Close... Enc ... count... ers... of... the... Third... Kind." They'll probably change the title. Nobody will be able to remember it.

I ask for a script again. My agent says Spielberg doesn't want anyone to see it for a while; he's afraid it will get ripped off for a movie for television. I am negotiating to spend twenty weeks of my life in Outer Mongolia doing a movie I'm not allowed to read. My agent suggests I call Spielberg and ask him about the script. I do. Spielberg is very nice, and tells me how good he thinks I'll be in the movie. Already I like the script. He tells me that I will be part of a team of scientists who are going around investigating a UFO phenomenon. He says Truffaut will probably be doing the film. I call Dreyfuss immediately. I ask him if I should be in this movie. I can't decide. He tells me to stop being an idiot.

Lynnie and I discuss what it will be like to be separated for twenty weeks. We decide it will be impossible but worth it. I realize Spielberg has ordered me not to shave my beard but I'm supposed to start rehearsals tomorrow for the play version of *Catch-22*. I will have to play a World War II Army officer wearing a full beard. I call the director and try to explain. For opening night I will trim my beard very closely. Maybe the audience will think it's stubble.

## MARCH 27

It's two o'clock in the morning and I'm sound asleep. The phone rings. It's Dreyfuss. He's very upset. He wants me to do the movie, and he's heard from Columbia that my agent may blow the deal on *Close Encounters* over billing and money. I haven't heard about this. I try to remain calm. Richard says I'd better tell my agent to stop pushing because it would be a shame not to be in such a wonderful movie. Even though the movie is budgeted at twelve million dollars, all the money has to be spent on special effects, not people, he says.

I try to calm Richard. I tell him there's nothing to worry about. Of course my agent won't blow the deal. He's a very good agent. (This is a big movie, I think. A few dollars more or less couldn't really make a difference to them.) I'm very rational, and make great sense, and Richard is very relieved when he hangs up. I, however, am completely hysterical.

## APRIL 2

The script arrived today, by messenger. He almost fingerprinted me before he'd let me sign for it. A cover letter from Columbia urges me to carefully destroy the old script when I receive a rewritten one. I sit down and start to read.

A warning on the first page orders me not to show the script to anyone, implying death by fire if I do.

The script starts with Neary at home with his family, fooling around with a train set. Suddenly the lights go out. Cut to little Barry in his room — all of his toys start to come to life. I'm sitting in my kitchen at two o'clock in the afternoon, and I'm absolutely terrified. I read the script in about an hour.

I call Spielberg and tell him how wonderful I think it is. He's really happy to hear my reaction.

This is exactly the kind of movie I have longed to be in since I first wanted to be an actor. It's a MOVIE movie, with chases, and a hero, and a spaceship at the end. I have to restrain myself from calling my agent and saying I'll do it for nothing.


**APRIL 5**

I get another 2:00 A.M. call from Dreyfuss. He tells me they are hiring some-one else, unless my agent gives in. I tell Dreyfuss I'm sure they're not doing that. He says they are. I ask him if Columbia knows he's getting on the phone and calling me about this. He says of course they do; they know I'm his friend. I say maybe that's why they're telling him these scary things. He says he never thought of that. He says goodbye, and tells me to go back to sleep.


**APRIL 8**

I give in a little, they give in a little, and we finalize the deal. I'm signing a contract tomorrow. I'm officially in *Close Encounters of the Third Kind.*


**APRIL 14**

I get a call from Spielberg. He's very excited I'm doing the movie, and wants me to meet him at his hotel to do some work with an interpreter. He wants to see whether his idea about my simultaneously translating while Truffaut speaks really works. I fear this is a test to see if I can *really* speak French. I hang up, and immediately begin reciting 'The Ant and The Grasshopper' to perfect my accent: "La cigale ayant chanté tout l'été ce trouva fort dépourvu..."

## APRIL 15

I walk into Spielberg's suite at the Sherry-Netherland Hotel. I try to appear calm, but I have been worrying ever since he called. I notice an attractive, red-haired, unmistakably French-looking lady on the couch, and a box of Danish butter cookies on a coffee table. I begin a conversation about the cookies, since I'd rather talk to Spielberg about the cookies in English than to the lady about the movie in French, but I quickly run out of conversation.

Spielberg says Truffaut has definitely committed to do the film, and I tell him how excited I'll be to work with him. I do not say how terrified I'll be.

Spielberg introduces me to the French lady, Françoise Forget, a Columbia interpreter. She will serve as the interpreter on location for Truffaut, should all things work out. He hands me a page from the script and suggests we read a scene from the movie together to hear what the simultaneous translation sounds like. It's in English. I speak English. Françoise Forget must translate my dialogue into French; while she is saying the lines in French I will overlap her in English. I notice that she is looking very nervous, and realize that Spielberg isn't auditioning me — he's auditioning *her.* I relax. This poor lady has to translate technical phrases which simply do not have French equivalents. Like: "Do a photogrammatic analysis of the northern face." She struggles valiantly. There is something about speaking the two languages at the same time that is extremely impressive and authoritative, and Spielberg is glowing. He really likes the way it sounds, and I'm glad because now in the movie I get to say everything anyone says in English in French for Truffaut, and I translate everything Truffaut says in French into English. My part has just doubled.

I decided I had better stop being so scared around Spielberg. I tell him that I've got some ideas for my part, and he tells me please to call him with them. He is especially interested in developing a new scene between Truffaut and me which expands our personal relationship, and I tell him that I will work on that. I grab one of his butter cookies as I get up to leave. I think I'll like being in this movie.

## APRIL 19

Went to Berlitz to sign up for French lessons today. I need someone to translate my part into French and then tell me how to pronounce everything. I would also like a complete grammar and vocabulary review. I want to revive my high-school French and speak fluently by the time the movie begins. I have three weeks to do this. The lady behind the desk tells me she has someone who specializes in exactly what I need. She takes me up to a multi-lingual instructor who worked with Robert De Niro on his Italian for *Godfather II*. He's sure he can help me.

We must translate the script into French before we can do any conversational work. I hand him the script and I tell him the movie is top-secret; he is not to reveal the plot to anyone. This man had no intention of telling anybody about the movie, but I'm sure my warnings have piqued his interest, and he'll probably be on the phone with Rona Barrett tonight.

He opens the script and we begin. "Go to the dark side of the Moon." He doesn't know what that means. He says that some of the lines have no literal French translation, so he teaches me to say "Fly to the part of the Moon you can't see." He has a terrible time with: "If they're not off the mountain by 0800 hours dust the northern face with E-Z-4." Finally, we get through about four pages and my first hour is up. I realize that I have spent all my time translating the script. I do not speak French one iota better than I did when I arrived.

Where is Miss Bessant now that I need her?

**THURSDAY, MAY 13**

I get a call from Shari Rhodes in Julia Phillips' office. She is frantic. Steven has changed the schedules. I am now the 'cover set' on Monday; if it rains, I'll work. I must be in Gillette, Wyoming on Sunday, May 16. But I can't be in Gillette since I'll be closing in *Catch-22* on Sunday, May 16. Shari is frantic. If it rains and I'm not there it will cost $50,000. She asks if I would be willing to leave for Wyoming immediately after my play closes; she says they will send a limousine to the theater to take me to the airport. She cajoles me into taking the grueling fourteen-hour night route to Wyoming. I'll spend the time conjugating French verbs.

**MAY 16**

The play has just ended. The limousine is waiting in front of the theater, and people are peering into it to see who's inside. No one is. I'm late.

I say goodbye to my friends. When I finally get to the limousine, the driver is very nervous. He knows that if I'm not on the 12:30 A.M. flight for Wyoming the movie can't start shooting tomorrow, and he feels personally responsible. The driver tells me to hurry.

I pile into the car with enough luggage for months. I'm bringing most of my clothes to Gillette because I had no time to go to Los Angeles for wardrobe fittings. We start driving. I have been very cavalier about getting to the airport on time, but it suddenly dawns on me that I could actually miss the plane. Steven Spielberg, François Truffaut, Richard Dreyfuss and a cast of thousands will be waiting in Wyoming for Bob Balaban who missed his plane. I start worrying along with the driver, and the two of us curse every red light until we finally get to the airport about ten minutes ahead of take-off. I race to the gate. I'm carrying a giant box of sandwiches and my Berlitz cassettes. I must go over my French for tomorrow in case it rains and I work. I board the plane and start going over my lines. I try not to think about what it will be like to meet François Truffaut. I rehearse some traditional French greetings.

We change planes in Chicago and fly to Minneapolis, where I have a four-hour wait for my connection to South Dakota. It's four o'clock in the morning and all the shops in the airport are closed, so I take my sandwiches and my cassettes and go to sleep in the waiting room next to gate four. I hope somebody wakes me when it's time to leave.

We change to a two-engine plane in Pierre. As we're going further West, our planes are getting smaller. By the time we reach Gillette we'll probably be travelling by helicopter. I have written postcards to everyone I know, and called the weather in Gillette four times. It says partly cloudy, chance of rain. By the time we land in Rapid City my legs are shaking and my eyes are closing. I've gone through fourteen hours of torture to be here in case of bad weather.

It is, of course, a gorgeously sunny day.

Dreyfuss, filming his approach to Devil's Tower.

# GILLETTE, WYOMING

**MAY 17**

*First day in Wyoming.* I'm exhausted and have a terrible headache. Finally got my bags, and am picked up at the tiny airport by a local driver from the movie. We start out for Gillette, which is two hours from the airport. He explains that we're going to the hotel, which is then an hour and a half from location.

The countryside is beautiful. Rolling hills, and lots of deer grazing. We drive for miles without seeing another car. It's warm out. The driver explains that last week the temperature suddenly started dropping, and there were snowflurries. He says the weather is unpredictable here. He tells me that I'll be able to see Devil's Tower way in the distance if I look really hard. I stare and keep thinking I see it, but the driver says I'm wrong. He says I'll know it when I see it.

I see a lot of signs pointing to Mount Rushmore and decide to try and get there on my day off. We keep driving; I try not to fall asleep. Finally, we near Gillette. Evidently I've missed the Tower. The green countryside turns to brown and trailer parks line the road. The driver explains that the construction industry can't catch up with the need for houses here, so most people live in trailers. We seem to be entering the heart of town, a main drag with lots of motels, bowling alleys and Denny's Restaurants. There are oil rigs everywhere. There's an IHOP and a Burger King, and no sidewalks. We pull into our two-story, slightly battered motel and I start unloading. Truffaut is staying here, but I don't see him. I imagine how strange it would be to run into François Truffaut at the ice machine.

The driver takes me to the location. We drive past more motels, bars and hamburger stands until we're in countryside again. We pass through small canyons and rocky cliffs. The driver says I'll be able to see the Tower as soon as we turn the corner. We make a sharp right and I can't believe what I see.

Devil's Tower looms ahead about fifteen miles in the distance, nine hundred feet of natural volcanic rock stretching straight up. It's a mammoth rectangle that stands out against the blue Wyoming sky as if it has been drawn on with a fine line marker. It's a very powerful sight.

I have been told that the studio wanted Spielberg to film all the Wyoming sequences at the Columbia ranch, a small patch of dirt and hills about a quarter of a mile down the road from the main studio buildings. I can see instantly why Steven chose Devil's Tower as a landing site for the Mothership, instead.

Further on, about ten miles from the Tower, hundreds of cars are creating a traffic jam. Trailers and lights are set up. Way in the distance, next to the camera, Steven is talking with Richard. I go over to say hello. I immediately notice that Richard looks very tired, and has a few days' growth. It doesn't dawn on me for a while that he has been made up to look this way. He is filming his arrival at Devil's Tower, and has spent the whole morning driving against traffic. It's been a difficult shot. Dreyfuss is very nearsighted. His character doesn't wear glasses, and Richard doesn't wear contact lenses. He has to take off his glasses as he drives the car, and he can't see a thing. He has been driving across the mountainous terrain, trying to keep his car on the road. Steven tells me that Nick McLean, the camera operator, was stationed on the hood of the car filming, and he didn't realize how blind Richard really was without his glasses. At one point, he was so scared that he insisted he be fastened more securely onto the hood of the car and that Richard drive more slowly.

Spielberg tells me to come by and watch a movie tonight. Richard and Spielberg have Winnebagos at the base of Devil's Tower so they don't have to get up early to drive to the location. They even have a cook out there. He's supposed to be very good, but he is having a hard time finding fresh vegetables. Truffaut was given one of the trailers too, but he didn't like staying in the woods, so he's back at the motel.

I go to wardrobe and try on my costumes. Nothing fits. They don't have thirty-six short. We all decide I will wear my own suits. The costume guy says it's a shame he didn't tell me to bring shoes.

---

**P.M.**

Having dinner with François Truffaut and his translator tonight to speak about our scenes. I hope I'm too tired to be nervous. I leave my clothes in a wardrobe truck and get driven back to the motel around 4:30. I unpack some more and wait for a call from Truffaut.

At around six, Françoise Forget, the Columbia interpreter, calls and says Truffaut wants to meet me in the lobby. I hurry over. Truffaut looks very stern. I am nervous and very quiet. I suggest we have dinner at a restaurant about half a mile down the gravel road behind our motel. Truffaut says he hopes they don't have loud music in the restaurant. I seem to be able to understand him. As we walk, I try to: (a) think of anything to say, and (b) speak French. I can do neither. I do a lot of nodding, but it's pitch black out so Truffaut doesn't even see me.

We get to the restaurant. A country and western band is blaring. We take one look, turn around, and make the long walk back to the hotel again. All I can think of to say to Truffaut is that it's nice to meet him. I say this over and over again. I feel like a total idiot. We get to our hotel dining room.

We're more relaxed, and dinner is actually fun. We make a lot of jokes about the steam table. All the food is "chicken-fried". It is impossible to translate chicken-fried steak into meaningful French.

Truffaut seems nice. He keeps asking for vegetables, and the sad little waitress keeps saying, "We have cottage cheese." I, of course, speak my normally fluent English to the waitress, who thinks I am French, too, and keeps repeating everything I say in English, in English. I tell Truffaut about my theatrical background. I tell him that my grandfather was a Hollywood producer who discovered Esther Williams. Truffaut loves to talk about the old Hollywood studios. He thinks that New York writers were very snobbish about their attitude towards Hollywood, and says Hollywood studios have produced a lot of good movies. He also says he is writing a book about actors, and he figures working for Spielberg is a great way to do some first-hand research.

After we finish ordering, I take out my script because I assume we're supposed to begin working. Truffaut looks very shocked and says we're not going to work until *after* dinner. I say I am very embarrassed. I feel like a social misfit. He laughs. I'm starting to like him. After dinner we go back to the lobby to work a little. We read a scene together. Truffaut is a terrific actor and makes me smile when he speaks English. He says he would love to speak English as well as I speak French. This is the perfect thing to say to me. I don't believe him.

**MAY 18**

I'm staying in Gillette today. I haven't worked yet. We're still waiting for it to rain. I didn't sleep well. I kept thinking I heard thunder so I went over my lines. This morning I'm exhausted, and of course the sun is shining.

I go into town to buy shoes for the movie. There's a strip of about five blocks of stores and diners. That's called downtown. You can tell it's downtown because it has sidewalks. There are a lot of western stores and, surprisingly, a couple of Chinese restaurants. The shoe store is so small that they only have one pair of shoes in each style, so you ask for your size, and they show you that one pair, and if you like it you buy it.

The food here is terrible. I go and buy food at the local supermarket and take it back to my room to eat. A wise choice.

**MAY 19**

Made the long bumpy ride to Devil's Tower again this morning. Truffaut and I work today. Finally. We will walk out of a Quonset hut and follow Neary

(Dreyfuss) as he is put into a waiting helicopter and sent away from the Tower with the other visionaries. Richard will have to scream and be all worked up. Fortunately, Truffaut and I don't have to say anything, which gives us a chance to get over first day jitters. I see the Tower in the distance again, and it looks even bigger than the other day. It looks like they built it for the movie — very one-dimensional.

At the foot of the Tower, Joe Alves, the Production Designer, has constructed the Government Evacuation Center, which we call the base camp. All the daylight scenes at Devil's Tower will be shot in and around this area. There are a lot of official-looking Army buildings, and trucks everywhere that say Piggly Wiggly and Baskin-Robbins on them. I assume they are bringing food for the extras, but I find out later they are prop trucks for the movie. All of our 'space' gear is supposedly camouflaged in them. There's a little A-frame restaurant in the middle of the park. The movie has put a big sign over it saying "Decontamination Camp". It has great root-beer floats.

Our honeywagons are lined up near a log cabin where the souvenir store owners live. I'm not sure why they call dressing trailers honeywagons. Somebody once told me it's because they have built-in portable bathrooms that attract flies like honey. I hope this isn't true.

I watch for a while as Steven rehearses with some visionaries in the helicopter. He reminds everyone to yell as though the propeller blades are turning, which they're not. Several crew members hold on to the sides of the helicopter and shake it back and forth to simulate the action of the blades.

Lance Henriksen, who's also in the scene, is very nervous today. He comes up to me and tries to establish a relationship "in character." He says I come from Harvard. That's fine with me. Ten extras come by dressed as giant bunnies. They are wearing decontamination suits with white hoods and fluffy white boots. I expect them to start singing, "Heigh ho, heigh ho..." François and I will have to wear these suits, too. François has wisely had his impeccably tailored. They tell me I will have to wear mine off the rack. I wish I were a famous French director.

I decide not to eat the movie breakfast (donuts), and go to the Totem Pole Gift Shop and order a frozen cheeseburger they heat in a microwave oven. I take it back to the honeywagons and chat with François. We're very anxious to work.

Small problem. Many of the extras (locals) have found beer and are getting drunk. They are fired, but it will be very hard to find replacements — because of the tremendous mining activity, there is almost no unemployment in Gillette. After a lot of frantic searching, they round up enough people who are willing to: (a) schlepp up to the Tower, and (b) cut their hair to look like Army guys. Steven is juggling shots to avoid seeing the crowd. Or lack of it.

**Miscellany:**

... Bob Westmoreland, the makeup man, comes around to cover our sunburned noses. He and Dreyfuss are great poker buddies. Bob's a member of the Screen Actors' Guild, as well, and as he's patting the makeup on your face, he reminds you that he wants to be an actor. Richard says he's actually a very good actor.

---

... Willy, a fabulous fifty year-old lady driver, runs around saying sentences with "vehicle" thrown in. "They've taken my *vehicle*, or I'd get you a fried egg sandwich,"... or, "Hey, will someone move those *vehicles* over there..."

---

... An extra dressed in an Army uniform thinks I'm Dreyfuss, and wants to know all about the shark in *Jaws*, I tell him it had big teeth and he goes away happy.

---

... François just sent a postcard to his youngest daughter in France. He says she loves to shop. François wrote her that she could spend all day shopping in Gillette and not spend ten dollars... Dreyfuss comes over to me and shows me the digital watch he wears in the movie. It doesn't read out the time until you press a button. A neat way of wearing a watch and solving continuity problems.

---

Had another chat with François. He mentioned again how fluently I speak French, and I told him he had won a place in my heart. It's very easy to talk with him. He's always joking and is very funny. Today, he told me he was going to have his head shaved, but he was only kidding. Unless I misunderstood the verb. François says that he saw beautiful storyboards for the end of the movie. He tells me how they will produce the special cloud effects that will appear throughout the film. They will drop white paint into water and oil, and project and photograph the results. He says he's heard the set for the end sequence where we meet the Mothership is fantastic. It's being built in Mobile, Alabama, because there isn't a soundstage big enough to hold it in Hollywood. I hear they turned down the Astrodome (too expensive) and a Goodyear Blimp Hangar (too small). We can't wait to see it.

It started to rain at 5:00 P.M. It's too late in the day to begin our cover set, so they send us home. As I get ready to go to the hotel dining room again, the AD calls saying there's a change in the schedule. We are doing a scene tomorrow that we weren't supposed to do until the end of the week, and I'm not prepared. I take out my script and start frantically going over my lines to memorize the French. I bring my pages to dinner tonight, and ask François' help with pronunciation. Order a hamburger which tastes funny, so I send it back. The waitress comes over later and says, "I told the cook I thought the meat had turned, and he said he could believe it."

## MAY 20

I don't know my lines as well as I should. I go over the scene with François and he says my pronunciation is terrific, but I can tell I'll have a hard time remembering what to say. I'll be spouting a lot of dialogue about spreading a sleep gas to trap Richard and Melinda as they run up the Tower, and I have a lot of lines like "This was a perfect strategic vacuum until he siphoned air into it," which are impossible for me to remember in French. I remind myself that Steven has another shot before our scene and I probably won't work until way after lunch.

Panic. An extra who was established in a shot yesterday never showed up for shooting today. They try to find him but he doesn't have a telephone. Suddenly François and I are the next shot. They rev up our helicopter and rush us into wardrobe. We do a rehearsal. I can barely remember my lines. Steven has stationed us directly in front of a helicopter that will actually take off during the scene. When it does, François and I are practically blown off our feet. I realize that every time I forget my lines, the poor man flying the helicopter will have to land his machine and start all over again.

We start filming. The helicopter takes off and François and I sway in the wind. Jeeps and extras are running about behind us, François says his last line, "They belong here more than we" (which is written on a large white cue card out of frame), and Steven yells "Cut!" We set up for another take. Steven says we almost got it right. In the second take I am more relaxed, but I forget all my lines. I mutter incoherently in broken French as helicopters and a hundred extras fly about. Steven runs up to us and says it went beautifully, and it's a wrap. I tell him that what I was saying made no sense at all, and we do another take. The next take, I'm OK but François looks down at his mark. We do three more takes until we finally get everything right.

We film the ride in the helicopter that will take Truffaut and me to the UFO landing field on the other side of Devil's Tower. We've had to wait for dusk since it is supposed to be dark when we reach the other side of the

SPIELBERG, TRUFFAUT & ME

mountain. Steven has told François and me to improvise a little something at the door of the helicopter. It's not the easiest thing in the world for me to improvise in English while entering a whirring helicopter. In French it's almost impossible. Steven senses my nervousness, and tells me we will take off, fly only a few feet, and land immediately. I decide that I will say to François something about having an extra scarf in my bag, in case it gets cold over there. I like that because it sounds conversational and seems like we're beginning to develop a relationship. The only trouble is that it's hard for me to remember the word for "scarf" — I keep saying the word for "tie," which makes my sentence totally ridiculous.

Steven tells me to yell during my closeup. He reminds me the helicopters are going. I hate yelling in French. François does his closeup and says his line very quietly. I think he has the right idea.

Steven films us closing the helicopter door and actually taking off. We don't rehearse, we just get into the helicopter and do it. The doors close, we try to fasten our seatbelts and I realize that we're not just going up a few feet and landing. We are a couple of hundred feet into the air, and we're banking steeply to the left. François is sitting next to the door. I'm squashed next to him, and neither of us can get our seat belts buckled. I look over and see that the door isn't latched properly and it's starting to open. An extra rushes over to hold it shut, and François and I are now a thousand feet up trying to hold on to our broken seat belts so we won't fall out of a door that won't close. We do this shot three more times.

---

As the sun goes down, it gets very cold at the Tower. We have to huddle near a giant arc light for warmth. Truffaut says he knows a joke I might like. He tells me a long, involved story about a Jewish girl who is engaged to be married. The punchline is something like "rich as Croesus" and "smart as Dreyfuss" and I have no idea what it means. He notices me not laughing and tries to explain why the joke is funny. He is very disappointed, as this is obviously one of his favorite jokes. I don't understand the joke but do realize it is about a Jewish girl, and I begin to fear that Truffaut is possibly anti-Semitic. He may find out that I'm Jewish and tell Spielberg how terrible my French is.

Later, Truffaut comes up to me. He had sensed I was worried about the joke, and could tell I thought he was being anti-Semitic. He says that of course the joke isn't, he isn't, and I'm very relieved.

**MAY 21**

Truffaut, Françoise Forget and I take a hike from the Tower to watch Steven filming shots of 'dead animals' in the road. According to the script, the animals have been placed there by the Government to look like poison gas is spreading in the area. I was concerned that they might really kill a lot of animals, but Steven has assured me no animals will be harmed.

A team of veterinarians is giving the animals shots of tranquilizers. Cows and sheep walk around drunkenly. Steven has to wait for them to sit on the ground and go to sleep. Then the vets arrange their legs and heads so the animals look dead instead of relaxed. They have to wait to film until one especially lively cow stops twitching her tail.

Every day at four o'clock, no matter what other shot we are doing, Dreyfuss, Melinda, Spielberg and the crew rush to the mountain to film the chase up Devil's Tower. The sequence can only be shot during the 'magic hours' of four to six o'clock, because the dusk has to match the dusk in the previous footage.

So everyone rushes to the mountain and spends a couple of hours climbing over enormous rock formations. Dreyfuss says he could never do this if he hadn't been working out for two months before the movie. Melinda is in a constant state of agony because she sprained her foot before the filming, and didn't tell anyone because she feared she'd be replaced. Her foot started to get better yesterday, but today when she jumps out of the helicopter to escape, she sprains it again. She keeps trying to look like she is not hopping as she runs up the mountain.

**MAY 22**

We're shooting at the base camp today. I act up a storm, and then realize that Steven has really been filming helicopters flying pre-fab toilets to the other side of Devil's Tower. I'm not sure we were even visible.

We're all getting very sunburned here. The makeup man says we have to be careful. It's cool out, but the altitude is so high that you get burned easily. We had lunch at the Decontamination Camp A-frame again, and François paid for me again, even though I tried to treat.

Had a talk with Dreyfuss about Truffaut. He says that he was intensely worried about meeting Truffaut because he is in such awe of his movies. The first day they met, Dreyfuss hadn't planned on meeting him. He just walked into Julia Phillips' office and Truffaut was sitting on the couch. Dreyfuss says he saw him and his mind slowly registered, "This... is...

François... Truffaut...” Truffaut saw Richard, and got up with his hand out-stretched, and Dreyfuss heard Julia Phillips say, “Oh, Richard, this is François Truffaut.” As Truffaut came forward, Dreyfuss kept waving his hands in front of his face saying, “Ohh noo... nooo... nooo...” Dreyfuss says he was so embarrassed that he has not yet recovered. The only thing he wants to say to Truffaut is, “I love you and I love your films!” Dreyfuss says he keeps finding himself rehearsing how to say “Good morning” to François and thinks this is not a good thing. Meanwhile, Truffaut keeps telling me how nice and talented he thinks Richard is. I keep telling this to Dreyfuss who refuses to believe me.

On our way back to the motel, we stop in a little town called Moorcroft to look at the rushes from the past ten days. No one has seen any of this film before, not even Steven or the Columbia executives, and everybody’s very excited. We have to drive very slowly, because Moorcroft is a speed trap, and four or five drivers from the movie have already gotten tickets. We arrive at a local church that has a makeshift movie theater set up in its recreation center. There’s even a popcorn machine.

We are all very anxious to see this film. The lights go out and the film comes on. It looks beautiful. In fact, Steven worries that the scenery looks too pretty and not foreboding enough. We look at a lot of shots establishing Richard’s breakneck drive through the evacuees near Devil’s Tower. We see Richard in his car drinking a Coke, and trying to follow a map as he swerves to avoid the traffic headed in his direction. We watch seven or eight takes of Richard arranging his map and trying to drive; in each take he manages to do something funny.

And then the film breaks. Steven’s assistant, Rick Fields, fixes it and starts the projector again. Then, after about a minute and a half, the sound goes out. Rick tries to fix it, and some of the camera crew go into the booth to see if they can help, but after fifteen minutes of frustrating starting and stop-ping, it’s apparent that there’s no way to fix the projector, and no way to buy a new tube in Moorcroft at eight o’clock in the evening. We watch about an hour of soundless rushes, then go dejectedly back to the hotel, leaving Steven to watch another two hours of the silent film.

## MAY 24

It’s the last day of the chase up Devil’s Tower. We’ve been filming it every afternoon for the last two weeks. Spielberg wants it to get darker during the sequence so by the time Dreyfuss and Melinda reach the top of the moun-tain and look down at us, it’s night. They’ve been filming closer to actual nightfall every day. Today they were at the top of the mountain when it got pitch black. Sixty people with a ton of cameras and lighting equipment had to pick their way back down the rocky mountain in total darkness. Dreyfuss says he's surprised everybody made it.

## MAY 25

I met Roger today. He is a member of the Parks Commission and has been stationed at Devil's Tower with his wife for the last five years. I call him Roger the Ranger. He looks like Smokey the Bear without the fur. He loves his Tower and is very afraid that if the movie is a big hit there will be an influx of tourists. He does not like tourists. I always thought that National Monuments were supposed to have a lot of tourists, but Roger explains that tourists litter. Sometimes they come to climb the tower, and he especially doesn't like that.

There is a prairie dog town at the foot of the Tower, and Walt Disney did some filming there for his famous prairie dog feature, *Perry*. I love prairie dogs. Roger says that sometimes tourists feed the prairie dogs. If they eat too many handouts they lose their desire to forage for food and don't store enough for the long cold winter months when there are no tourists. I am beginning to understand why Roger doesn't like tourists.

I bring Truffaut over to see the prairie dogs. He has no interest in seeing them, but finally goes because I want him to so much. At first all the prairie dogs stay in their holes, and I am embarrassed because Truffaut doesn't want to be here in the first place. Finally, a few peek out shyly at us. They bark their high bark, and some mothers come out of their holes followed by tiny little prairie dog children. Truffaut enjoys seeing them. I walk closer to one of the dogs to get a better look, and he notices me. How odd, I think, that he doesn't run away. He hops a few steps closer to get a better look at me. I back up a little, and the little animal advances toward me more quickly. Truffaut laughs and says the prairie dog is in love with me. I am not laughing. The animal approaches at a rapid hop and I have to run to keep him at a distance. Truffaut thinks this is one of the funniest things he has ever seen.

We leave the prairie dog town. Truffaut is walking. I am running down the hill, my enamoured prairie dog trying desperately to keep up with me.

---

**Miscellany:**

... Melinda and Richard film a scene where they race their car cross-country and hurtle through a barbed wire barricade on their way to Devil's Tower. Melinda and Richard are not really in the car, however. Spielberg is using stunt doubles because the terrain is rough, and the car could easily flip over. On the third take, the car rips through the fence and sends barbed wire snaking out around the camera crew. One of the grips gets caught in about ten feet of wire, and is dragged along the ground until someone screams for the car to stop. Miraculously, he is unharmed. He is wearing a very heavy leather jacket, and the wire has not quite eaten its way through to his skin. He could have been cut in two. We all move back about twenty feet for the next take.

---

... After work, we all go to the 'Gay 90s Steak House'. François didn't come because there's loud music. A sign on the door says "Men must wear shirts and remove hats while dining or dancing." Strange place, Gillette. Its main claim to fame (pre-*CE3K*) is the largest strip mine in the country, which sits like an open wound a couple of miles outside of town. They're running a contest in the local paper to name the mine. Gillette is a real frontier town, and everyone's cashing in on the mining dollars. Five-room shacks in the middle of sand patches are selling for $75,000, and even at that price they're hard to find. It's a testimony to Julia Phillips' ingenuity that she has located a fleet of limousines in this wilderness for the visiting Columbia executives.

**MAY 26**

Truffaut and I go into the Devil's Tower Trading Post to buy some souvenirs. There is a tremendous assortment: salt and pepper shakers, pennants, china figures and those smelly carved log statues you get at the Grand Canyon. Everything is marked 'Devil's Tower'. Truffaut buys a pennant and I buy some commemorative plates with the 'Legend of the Tower' printed on them: "Indians, fleeing an attack by a neighboring Tribe, made their camp on the side of the Tower. In the morning they awoke to find themselves sur-rounded by packs of ferocious wolves. They would have been eaten alive, but the Spirit took pity on them and suddenly pushed them high up away from danger..." Interesting. I pick up another plate: "Devil's Tower came into being when a brave Warrior died and his grieving Maiden prayed for the Spirit to take him to the Happy Hunting Ground, and the mountain heard, took pity and raised him closer to the heavens."

We pack up the souvenirs and go outside. A group of small children have gathered to watch a helicopter carrying more equipment to the far side of the Tower. Truffaut notices some kids sitting on the curb of a gas station. He smiles and walks over to them and says hello. He looks so friendly that even though they don't understand what he is saying, he is instantly accepted as one of them. He sits down with the kids. One of them begins throwing stones to see if he can hit an old Mounds wrapper, and Truffaut joins him in a contest. They spend the afternoon sitting there, watching helicopters, and trying to hit the candy wrapper with little pebbles. Truffaut tells me later how much he loves to film small children. He says when you photograph a child you have a record of something that will never be duplicated. Everything children do is spontaneous; they are incapable of repetition.

He describes a scene from his new movie *Small Change* in which a little girl, left at home by her parents, runs to the window and shouts after them. The little girl he hired became suddenly shy when it was time to film the scene, and couldn't talk above a whisper. It was crucial for the scene to have her yelling out the window, and Truffaut didn't know what to do. He got an idea. He had the girl pick up a bullhorn from a chair, go to the window, and speak into it to her parents. The machine was turned all the way up, so no matter how softly the girl talked, her voice boomed loudly. Later, Truffaut changed the profession of the girl's father, so that he could logically have a bullhorn in his house.

We both are eager to work on the Big Set in Mobile. I tell Truffaut I've heard that Steven is looking for little girls who are expert rollerskaters to play the extraterrestrials. (I have to dig up Forget to say the word for "rollerskates".) They will glide from the ship on the rollerskates but will be shot from the ankles up, so they will appear to be floating. The Martian roller derby.

## MAY 27

It's the big Major Walsh scene today, in which Lacombe (Truffaut) and I try to convince Major Walsh that Neary should be allowed to go to the far side of the mountain and watch the UFO land.

François and I go over the scene in the car on the way to Devil's Tower. He is as worried about remembering his lines in English as I am about remembering my lines in French. We try to help each other. We arrive and Steven is still asleep in his trailer, so we change and get made up. I have my bald spot painted brown. Steven gets up and we rehearse the scene. It goes well. Steven wants me to be more agitated. We wait until 12:30 for the crew to set up the lights in our Quonset hut, and then go inside for a rehearsal on the set. It is about a hundred degrees inside. Someone says this is nothing compared to Mobile.

François is nervous about the scene. He writes his lines on manila envelopes and frantically tapes them to the walls, the camera, and finally on to Major Walsh's chest. We film. I try to convince Major Walsh that Neary really belongs here, and François and I make an impassioned plea to let this little group with the 'Implanted Vision' remain at the Tower. François has a line, "This is a small group of people." He keeps saying, "This is a small people." So finally Steven decides to have François say the line in French and have me translate it into English. We get to the part where François implores Major Walsh to let Neary stay. I get so carried away that I have to keep stopping myself because I am translating things that François hasn't said yet. After what seems like a thousand takes, Steven keeps wanting it louder and faster, and we're very hot and very tired. Steven asks François to yell, and he tries, then apologizes, saying he is as loud as he can be; he's really a very quiet person. Later, François says that he is only slightly more aggressive than I. I go into an immediate tailspin, because I think I have been acting very aggressively lately.

---

**Miscellany:**

> ROGER THE RANGER MEETS SAMUEL BECKETT: In the script, the government has closed the Tower because of a phony nerve gas leak, so Joe Alves wants to put up a big prop sign near the Tower saying, "Closed". Roger the Ranger says they can't close the park; it's open to the public year-round. Joe says, "We're not really closing the park, we're just putting up a sign *saying* it's closed." Roger says, "But the sign says it's *closed*," and Joe says, "It's not really a sign, it's just an illusion of a sign," and on they go.

---

Steven has to match a shot which was begun on a cloudy day, so we're waiting for the sun to go behind a cloud. Steven and the crew have just come from watching rushes of our big helicopter scene. Steven thought the moment where François said, "They belong here more than we" was really lovely, but he says he wants the line in English, so he will subtitle it. Someone tells him the line *was* in English. The big joke today is when François speaks English, it sounds like French. Buddy Joe Hooker, the stunt coordinator, rushes up to François and says the line in pigeon English: "Zay bee-long ere Mozambique." Truffaut loves it, and yells back, "Tudore yellou tchevrolay coupay" which I am finally able to translate as "two-door yellow Chevrolet coupé." Later Buddy Joe comes by with T-shirts with "Zay bee-long ere Mozambique" printed on the back.

On the Crescendo Summit set in Mobile.

# MOBILE, ALABAMA

**MAY 28**

Friday. Goodbye Gillette. We make the drive to Rapid City past Mount Rushmore, which I never did get to see, although Steven had a helicopter pick him up from location this morning and make a quick circle around it on his way to the airport. A possible homage to Hitchcock? We gather in the coffee shop and wait for the chartered plane that will take us to Mobile, Alabama. I can't wait to see the "Big Set". Everybody's been building it up so much I hope it's not a disappointment.

Our plane is ready to board, and the entire cast and crew of *CE3K* pile into the rented 727. I wonder who will get to sit in tourist and who will be in first class. The stewardesses are thrilled to be on a "movie plane". It occurs to me that a rival studio could easily finish off Columbia with one well-placed bomb. As we take off, I notice I have absolutely no fear of flying. God wouldn't dare to do anything to all these famous, rich people.

Julia Phillips' two year-old daughter Kate comes over to say hello, and we play with my tape recorder for a few minutes. The stewardess asks for our attention. She has an announcement to make. I assume she'll tell us something about the Grand Canyon. She says that Julia and Michael Phillips' film *Taxi Driver* just won the award for Best Film at the Cannes Film Festival. We applaud wildly, and the stewardesses pass around champagne.

---

I can see Mobile below. It looks green and civilized, and the streets have sidewalks. I'm very glad not to be in Wyoming anymore. As we land, I hear some of the crew making plans to go over to the Big Set. I feel like I've just come back from eight weeks at summer camp.

We get off the plane, we're hit in the face by a blast of unbelievably hot, humid air.

We drive to our hotels. I check in to the downtown Holiday Inn, and immediately unpack everything I've brought along for the months ahead: clothes, books, tape recorder, record player, and Bullworker Exerciser. I'm going to be here a long time and the room is really depressing; I better move somewhere else. I go to the lounge and play a few Pong games. Very badly. Nick, the camera operator, says Dreyfuss was in earlier tonight and was unbeaten at the same Pong game I cannot make move from left to right.

Everyone is talking about what it will be like to work on what is now officially called the "Big Set".

Dreyfuss had heard that the hangar is so big and will be so intensely hot, that when they turn on the air-conditioning, cold dry air will meet warm, moist air, and clouds will form somewhere near the roof and could produce rain. He speculated about the emotional and psychological effects of so many hundreds of people cooped up in a hot, humid enclosure. It doesn't sound good.

Crew members are filling the bar here; haven't been so many people in this place in years. Local girls are coming on to the crew members. They're dying to hear all about the "film". Looks like movie fever has hit Mobile.

## MAY 29

I arrive at the Big Set. It looks more like a General Motors plant than a movie studio. Hundreds of cars are parked in front of a gigantic airplane hangar. A tent-like structure covered with a white tarpaulin sticks out from its side. Joe Alves had this tarp specially made. It's white on the outside and black on the inside, so it will reflect the heat and still give the total blackness required for the special effects inside. Nobody figured there would be much of a problem building it. They figured they'd just sink some bolts into cement and string up a tarp, but when they called in the engineers they found that they'd have to dig a hole twelve feet deep, two feet wide, and 180 feet long and sink huge cement beams on which to anchor the ties. Joe specifically put the tarp to the lee side of the strong southern Gulf winds, and it's supposed to be hurricane-proof.

There is tremendous security around the complex. First we get cleared by a guard in a sentry booth near the entrance. As we go into the building, another guard comes over to me and asks to see my ID badge. I don't have one, so I go into a little room and have a Polaroid picture taken. It's put on a laminated plastic card which I am told to wear when entering the hangar. The card has my name underneath. I am given another laminated card. This one has the same picture, but underneath is the name of my character, David Laughlin. I am told to bring that to wardrobe and always wear it on my costume. I feel like I'm in *Mission: Impossible*.

I enter a maze of offices where it is very cool. They've obviously been exaggerating how hot the set is. Secretaries behind partitions are handing out 'background cards' to a noisy line of eager-looking, potential extras. "Do you speak a foreign language?" "Do you have any special mechanical skills?" The phones are ringing with a steady stream of people who want to be in the movie. Mothers who have gotten the date wrong, are bringing their six year-old daughters to be interviewed for parts as extraterrestrials. All of Mobile wants to be in pictures.

I locate a production secretary behind some partitions and tell her I want to move from my hotel. She gives me a list of unpromising-looking alternatives, and I ask directions to the set. I am sent down a winding corridor past a Xerox room and a lot of closed doors, but I don't see anything that looks like a "Big Set". I find the makeup room, and go past a large dining area with steam tables set up where people are carving large roast beefs. I'm sure that in a few days I'll be able to find my way around easily, but right now I have a strong urge to drop breadcrumbs.

I finally locate Steven who takes François, me and some others on a tour of the set. He leads us down the long corridor I've already passed through, and explains that the set is at the core of the complex we're in. We must be getting closer, because it's getting warmer. We're all in a great state of anticipation.

Steven pushes open a large double door and tells us we're here. It's hot, but nothing unbearable. Steven says that's because the movie lights aren't on. It's very dark, and I can't make out much more than acres of black velvet drapes everywhere. Steven explains that the velvet is a backing that surrounds the set. Most of the special effects will be added in front of this black background after we finish filming. We will be in this room for the next two and a half months. The Mothership will land, and the extraterrestrials will have their first taste of Earth life right here in this hangar.

As my eyes adjust to the light, I see a lot of scaffolding supporting the backs of large fiberglass boulders. Steven leads us up a long flight of rickety stairs that zigzag towards a platform about halfway to the ceiling. It's a long hike and the stairs shake. We get off at the landing. I walk forward, and spread out below me is an astonishing sight: a long, concrete landing field stretches out for what looks like miles. It is surrounded by piles of rocks which look exactly like the rocks at the base of Devil's Tower. It's as if we never left Wyoming. Steven explains that the color, texture and shape of the rocks duplicate the Wyoming rocks exactly. Someone yells to us from the far end of the hangar, but he's so far away that I can't make out who it is. The whole panorama is awe-inspiring.

There is an enormous network of lights, grids, ladders and electrical cables that covers the ceiling. Gaffers are climbing around up there plugging and unplugging lights, but I can't look up any more because I'm getting dizzy.

Steven says he will start the filming from a platform another fifty feet above us, and then gradually work his way down to the ground. He needs to shoot a lot of coverage of us from very high angles to establish the point of view of the Mothership as it flies above us prior to landing. He will shoot the entire last sequence three times — once from each of the two platforms, and then from the ground floor. He says the view is really terrific up there, so we get back on to the ladder and climb almost another fifty feet. I try desperately not to look down. The stairs are really shaking now, and I hold on to the wooden support slats with both hands. Nobody else seems to mind.

Truffaut is fascinated by all of this. I try to translate for Steven, but my translation gets vaguer as my vertigo increases.

We arrive at the next level. The view is spectacular. Technicians working on the landing strip look like toy figures. The immensity of *Close Encounters* is hitting me for the first time. I flash on the souvenir program of *The Ten Commandments*: "It took fifty propmen two years to hold back the Red Sea..."

We pick our way downstairs, which is even more difficult than going up. We get to ground level, and we walk onto this Big Set. Two flags are waving at either end, an American flag and a French flag. Someone is adjusting fans to make them both wave in the same direction. Men are working in the ground command modules, and someone is trying to get the blue neon that runs along the center of the concrete straight. The set is so large that it doesn't feel like being on a set. I feel like I'm standing on a landing strip in the middle of a mountain.

Steven leads us through a side entrance, past the adjoining hangar where Joe Alves is building a mini-version of Devil's Tower for closeups, and up to another level with more offices. We pass through a room with hundreds of color renderings of the final special effects sequence of the movie. I had visualized a fantastic sequence when I read the script, but nothing like this. Extraordinary. Steven has drawn and numbered every shot. He says that rather than working from the script, he will refer to these pictures for the next months of shooting on the Big Set. We meet the artist who is sitting nearby in a little room behind a pile of sketches. He is busily drawing in little figures and bright lights, and tacking his renderings to a crowded bulletin board. As we talk, he continues to draw. Steven says the artist started almost a year ago, and he is still working eight hours a day illustrating the new things Steven constantly dreams up for the movie.

There is a model of the whole set in the corner of the room. It's beautiful. I ask Steven who gets to keep it after the movie. He says he does: it's in his contract. I tell him if he puts a piece of glass on it'll make a great coffee table.


**MAY 31**


We drive out to a Holiday Inn about twenty miles from the Holiday Inn we're already staying in. Evidently the grillwork on our Holiday Inn looks too Southern.

We're filming a sequence in which I get the news that plans to meet the Mothership are finalized, and I rush into François' room to tell him we'll be leaving for Devil's Tower immediately.*

Dozens of extras dressed as scientists are being drilled to bustle around the swimming pool carrying loads of books and documents. Some of the paying guests come over to us to complain. They can't use the swimming pool or they'll be in the shot. We've ruined their vacation. A woman recognizes me from an old *Mod Squad*, but wonders who François is. He tells her he is my agent.

We spend the morning filming me reading a computer printout, looking happy, and running down the corridor to François' room. This afternoon, we will film me entering his room. It's getting hot.

After lunch we move into François' crowded, stuffy room. Steven explains the scene to us. François will have just fallen asleep listening to English language cassettes ("Good morning."... "What a lovely frock you are wearing."). Steven got the idea to use these from François who has been studying English for years, and carries a cassette recorder everywhere trying to perfect his English. Steven is using François' actual English cassette. The scene is going well. I open the door quietly, tiptoe in and awaken François. We do endless versions of him waking up. The room is so small that there isn't even room for Françoise Forget so I'm doing the translating. It's getting hotter and stuffier, and I'm getting punchy. Steven asks me to tell François to get out of bed and put his feet on a mark on the floor. I tell François in my best French, and he laughs wildly. I have told him to get out of bed and put his feet on a mark on the ceiling. Thank God today is almost over.

We set up outside the room for a quick shot in which François watches the scientists preparing to leave for Devil's Tower.* Steven moves in for a closeup of François. He wants him to look at all these people getting ready to leave for our climactic meeting at the end of the film, and then look up at the sky for just a moment, anticipating the wonders ahead. We do a take.

François looks up. The effect is chilling. Steven says this is the first time in the filming he's had anyone look at the sky, and it's a very exciting moment for him. Originally his title for the movie was, *Watch the Skies*.

## JUNE 25

Just got back from a few weeks off in New York. I finally meet Teri Garr at the hotel coffee shop. We aren't in any scenes together, so every time she works, I get to go away and vice versa. Over stale Danish, she tells me that Spielberg decided to cast her after he saw her in an MJB coffee commercial. She kept wanting to play Jillian (Melinda's role), but Spielberg said she was so perfect in her coffee commercial, she had to be Neary's wife, the ultimate Middle American.

Before she started working, Spielberg gave her Bill Owen's book *Suburbia* and said to choose her wardrobe from it. When she shopped for her costumes, she refused to buy anything that wasn't polyester. In Mobile, this was not difficult. She also spent a week in Anaheim, living in her sister-in-law's tract home to observe daily life in a suburban town. To prepare for her part, she even went to Sears last week and pretended she was buying a set of maple bedroom furniture.

Since she's been in Mobile, Steven's been encouraging her to buy things for the house set, so she'll feel at home in it. Today, she put her own "chore charts" up on the refrigerator.

Yesterday, Teri spent a very long day doing the mashed potato scene: she and her three kids get very upset when Richard goes crazy and starts building Devil's Tower out of the mashed potatoes. She is impressed with Steven's attention to detail in that scene. She tells me that Steven carefully chose the menu for the meal: he ordered niblets, mashed potatoes (the kind that come from the package) and roast beef. It sounds better than the food at the hotel.

Teri says the kids have been terrific. One of them is Richard's nephew, Justin. Steven wanted him to be one of Richard's kids because he looks so much like Richard, but Justin said he'd rather play baseball. So Steven convinced him that he would have a wonderful time being in the movie. He is having a wonderful time. Every time Richard starts building his mashed potato mound, Justin laughs. It's a valid reaction, but not what Steven is looking for, so they had to do a lot of re-takes. The older boy, Steven Bishop, is an actor from New Orleans, and whenever Steven asks him to cry, tears just roll down his face. He has been able to do this all afternoon, and at one point Richard asked him how he does it. He says he just thinks of his dog and gets sad. Everyone is tremendously impressed. The little girl, Adrienne Campbell, is only three years old, so she doesn't really understand she's in a movie. She kept saying "There's a dead fly in my mashed potatoes," over and over, and Steven liked it so much he decided to keep it in. They're all exhausted because they've been filming in this overcrowded, very hot house for fourteen hours. No one will be ordering mashed potatoes for a very long time.

---

Spoke to Joe Alves about how he chose the house for the movie. He says he went to Muncie, Indiana to examine tract homes, then found a house near Mobile that looks like the houses in Muncie.

When he found the house he called Columbia and told them they should buy it. Since they were going to have to put in new lawns, rebuild the inside and eventually cut a wall for camera access, he figured it would be cheaper to own it. Columbia wouldn't buy it, so Joe and Clark Paylow, the unit manager, decided they'd buy it themselves and rent it to Columbia and then sell the house at a profit after all the improvements. They told Columbia they were going to do this. Columbia then decided to buy the house. They paid thirty-five thousand dollars for it, and everyone figures it'll go for over forty after shooting's completed. Not a bad deal.

They're making it a real middle-class, all-American home, complete with all the latest electrical appliances in shades of yellow and avocado, and a Kean painting over the piano. They've filled the house with cheap French Provincial furniture, and since Neary is a hobbyist, they've given Richard a den, complete with electric trains, woodworking kits, model airplanes — every hobby imaginable.

## JUNE 26

It's our first day of filming on the "Big Set".

It's very hot and very humid; they weren't exaggerating. Every time we shoot, three men carrying fog machines spray white mist everywhere. It's a lot like working in a rain cloud.

I don't have to worry about how I look for the next few weeks because Steven is filming from the highest platform, about a hundred feet up. I figure if I can't see him, he can't see me. The actors stand around and wait for assistant directors to yell into bullhorns and tell us where to move. I have no idea what we're doing. Steven is using a special lens that will make us look even smaller and farther away from the camera than we actually are. Later on, he will optically reduce our size even more. He'll fill in the surrounding Wyoming countryside using paintings and miniatures, so we will appear to be at the base of the actual Devil's Tower, instead of in the world's largest airplane hangar in Mobile. The shots will be used to establish the point of view of the Mothership as it comes sailing over the Tower.

I am carrying the briefcase I will hold for the next three months. I decide always to hold it in my left hand so I won't have to worry about matching. We break for lunch and file over to a large room behind the office area. Everyone's very pleased because we are exactly on schedule. Actually, Steven is two shots ahead, and everyone sees this as a great omen. I get in line with about forty cast and crew members and the cooks dish out the same plates of beef and mashed potatoes and green beans we ate in Gillette.

Four hundred extras file in after us. One comes over and asks my name. When I say Bob Balaban, he's very disappointed. He had bet another extra ten bucks that I was Richard Dreyfuss.

After lunch an AD announces the rules: there will be as much air-conditioning as possible, but we must bear with the producers, and not plan on being too cool for the next few months. There will be absolutely no smoking on the Big Set. It's very flammable. And no eating or making a mess of any kind. The Big Set is very expensive, and it shouldn't get dirty. I expect a list telling me how much underwear to bring, and what kind of name tapes to use.

I meet Richard's father, Norman Dreyfuss, who is visiting from Pasadena. I have deduced that he is a relative of Richard's because he looks just like me. Steven was looking for executive-types to work as extras, so Richard volunteered Norman. No one looks more 'executive' than Norman Dreyfuss. In between takes he pulls out his *Wall Street Journal* and studies it intently. Norman figures he'll spend a month or two in Mobile and just get away from it all. He has no idea how successfully he has done just that.

It's time to quit for the day. It doesn't feel like we've done anything but stand and eat, but Steven is four shots ahead of schedule and the crew is euphoric. Julia Phillips grabs a bullhorn and announces there will be a party at the back of the hangar to celebrate our first day on the Big Set. She reminds us to stay on the dirt surface at the rear and not to bring our drinks anywhere near the concrete landing area. There will be pink champagne for everyone. The extras cheer wildly. They had no idea being in a movie was this much fun. This is their first day.

## JUNE 29

We're doing more long shots establishing our positions on the base of the canyon for the Mothership sequence. Hundreds of extras playing the parts of technicians and scientists are being moved around like chess pieces. François and I aren't even visible in the shots so we're off for the morning. François goes to his office to do some work on a new screenplay, and I explore. I go over to the adjoining hangar to watch the Mothership being built. It's the large UFO that will bring the smaller UFOs and the extraterrestrials to Devil's Tower for the close encounter at the end of the film, and Steven has explained that while most of it will be inserted as special effects in post-production, the bottom, out of which the ETs will exit, will actually be constructed. And here it is. It's supposed to be ready next week, but its twenty tons of steel girders are still only half covered with black velvet and silver mylar.

Someone from the crew is applying colored gels to the inside of little rectangular windows that run along the top, and glueing strips of black velvet to the outside of the hull. It doesn't look like a 'saucer'. In fact, it's hard to make out its shape. Steven says he wants the ship to look big, but doesn't want it to have "hard edges". I wonder why it has to be made out of steel. Steven explains that since all sorts of special effects will be added around the outlines of the ship, it mustn't bend or waver during filming and steel girders are the only thing that will do the job.

The Mothership is sitting in front of a half-completed set for Crescendo Summit. The UFOs will be seen for the first time here, and Melinda Dillon will save Cary Guffey from being hit by Richard's truck on the road that runs through it. The Summit has real evergreen trees growing on it, and a maintenance man is climbing up the road watering them. Usually, plants on an indoor set start to die immediately, but it is so hot and humid inside this hangar that the greenery is doing beautifully. I ask the maintenance man if he thinks the Mothership will be finished on schedule. He says yes, because we have to be off the Big Set by the end of the month. I don't believe him.

I walk upstairs past Steven's office. A giant blowup of him sitting between two Devil's Tower prairie dogs fills an entire wall, and an original Buck Rogers ray gun sits on his desk enshrined in a plastic case.

Richard's dressing room is right next door. It's filled with furniture. He has about six different Pong games here, everything from 'Battleship' to 'Tank' to 'Gunfighter'. Sometimes he and Steven relax by playing the electronic games. He says they started playing together on *Jaws*, and now they're pretty evenly matched. As a matter of fact, about the only thing Richard doesn't have in his dressing room are plants. He says he doesn't believe in plants, and jokes that he likes to be the only living thing in the room.

---

Fifty six year-old girls have been hired to play extraterrestrials in the final sequence, and Susan Heldfond, their choreographer-keeper, is working with them in a rehearsal room. She is trying to get them to run in circles while shuffling their feet and waving their arms. She keeps yelling "quick little feet," but they're not really paying attention. Some are sitting down, some are wrestling in the corner, and a few are running around in circles. The girls were hired from local dancing schools. They had to be very little to fit into their costumes which are all the same size and were made long before the children were hired, but they also had to be old enough to follow instructions. They will play a crucial part in the climax of the movie, and at the $60,000 a day it will cost to film the sequence, the scene must go as smoothly and as quickly as possible.

I wonder whether Spielberg has stopped by to watch any of these rehearsals. Susan brings out the heads and the hands the kids will wear as ET. The heads look like giant fetuses and are really quite frightening; some kids start crying as soon as they see them. Spielberg has been working with Joe

Alves trying to come up with a head that looks other-worldly, but friendly. Work is still in progress.

After some coaxing, one brave little black girl puts on a head, and soon several of the kids are wearing heads and hands, and running around in circles. They keep bumping into each other because the eyeholes have been incorrectly placed, so Susan removes the heads and continues with running practice. Lunch is called, and the Mother In Charge leads the kids away. She looks a lot like Jayne Meadows and is a very pushy stage mother type. She is acting like this movie is her daughter's big break into show business, and I can't figure out why, since all the girls are exactly the same size, and will be indistinguishable in their rubber heads and hands.

In the room next door, a group of mimes in technicians' costumes are rehearsing slow-motion movement. Steven's plan is for the ETs to move very quickly, and, at the same time, for the mimes to move very slowly. He will film the scene at high speed. When the movie is shown, the mimes will appear to be moving normally, while the ETs will be moving with super-human quickness.*

---

**Miscellany:**

... We're doing more "standing around on Big Set and being filmed in the distance." I bring a lot of books and magazines, and I'm doing some writing, so I carry everything in my briefcase. Yesterday, Steven yelled, "Action!" and when I tried to stuff my things back into it, the case fell apart. Luckily the prop man had a duplicate.

---

... We're doing shots where we anxiously await a sign from the Mothership. We are about to look up at the sky and notice UFOs forming the Big Dipper. But whenever all the lights are turned on, something happens to the generator and there is total black-out. We have to wait for someone to fix the fuses.

---

... A fiftyish lady extra dressed as a scientist comes over to François. She says her son was really impressed to hear he was in the film and could she have his autograph. He obliges, and she asks François what it is exactly that he does.

---

... We go to the makeup room to wait. The makeup room has everything — a refrigerator, magazines, things to drink, even grapes. Steven stops in to check out some French phrases with me. He wants to learn enough French to be able to call to François during a take, and we go over words like, "slower", "faster" and "to the right".

---

... The makeup man comes by, very excited. Steven has decided he's right for a small part in the movie. He will be in the scene at Neary's power plant. He's already planning intricate makeup for the role and I can't figure out why, because he looks exactly like someone who works at a power plant.

---

... Heard today we're not going to Outer Mongolia. Something about difficulty in getting visas for everyone. I am relieved, because now I don't have to learn, "The sun came out last night and sang to us," in Mongolese.

---

... I've moved into a nice room at the Mobile Sheraton. I am happy now.

## JUNE 30

I ask Norman Dreyfuss how things are going in Mobile. He seems pretty bored. He's also very hot. He has decided to play the rest of his scenes in the command module with his jacket off and his sleeves rolled up. If Norman Dreyfuss is taking his jacket off, it must really be hot.

Richard says his father is very neat. The other day, as an experiment, he tried leaving some clothes on his bed, but after a couple of hours he couldn't stand it any longer and had to hang them up. Norman says Richard is not neat. He says that when he's at Richard's house he finds himself folding Richard's sweaters and straightening his closet.

---

Dreyfuss takes me to see *Jaws* tonight at a local movie theater. He and Spielberg can't believe I haven't already seen it. Dreyfuss says he wants to be there to see my reaction to it. He tells me I'll scream a lot. We get to the theater late, and as we're getting our popcorn two girls stop me and ask for my autograph. They've just seen the movie and they think I'm Dreyfuss, who has now shaved his beard and stopped wearing rimless glasses. I don't tell them I'm really me, and sign Richard's name. I love the movie, and scream in the right places, and Dreyfuss has a great time watching me watching him. As we exit the theater a couple of people come over to us and tell me I was great. I thank them, Richard laughs, and we leave.

## JULY 1

On the drive to the hangar this morning, Truffaut tells me he's learned a lot about actors from working on this movie. He says he's going to be much more patient with them in the future. Truffaut explains he had a line of dialogue to say yesterday that he's been worrying about for months. The line is "Einstein was right." He read it in the script last May and he's been worrying about it ever since. Will people laugh when he says it? How will he read the line? He's developed a real fixation about it. He's especially worried about finding a nice way to tell Spielberg that he doesn't want to say the line. And then he fears that Spielberg may want him to say it anyway, and then what will he do? He has been dreading the day the scene would be shot, and they finally got around to it yesterday. Truffaut says he was nervous all morning, preparing excuses for Spielberg, and when they got to the line in rehearsal Spielberg went over to another actor and gave the line to him. Truffaut says that instead of being relieved he said to himself, "Why has he given someone else my line?" He worried about it all afternoon.

## JULY 2

Night shooting, tonight. The scene promises to go on till dawn. Everyone's drinking a lot of coffee. We're filming the scene where Truffaut and I meet; we have come to the airport to investigate a commercial jet that has just flown past a UFO.* My character, Laughlin, has been hired to act as Truffaut's interpreter. During the scene, Truffaut quizzes me to make sure I can translate not just the words, but the emotional truths behind them. There is a lot of dialogue in the scene; we ask Steven if he minds us making some changes in the dialogue. He says no, so Truffaut and I rewrite some of our speeches. Then Truffaut types up the scene on his portable, non-electric typewriter. It's great to watch him type. He uses two fingers, but it's not hunt and peck; it's more like find and pound. I would recognize the sound of him typing anywhere. I'm collecting memorabilia from the movie like a pack rat, so before we leave, Truffaut and I gather up early drafts of the scene and stick them in my briefcase.

---

Lynnie is coming in tonight. Before they changed the schedule, we were going to have a romantic dinner by the sea. Now we will spend the evening waiting in a tiny portable dressing room. The only good thing is that we are shooting at the airport where her plane is landing, so at least I can pick her up. Spielberg decides to begin by filming a few shots in the interior of the jet, and already I can tell that Truffaut and I won't start work until after midnight. I go to meet Lynnie. She has been looking forward to meeting Truffaut for months, as he's her favorite director. Since she doesn't speak French, I've worked with her on some simple phrases like "It's a pleasure to make your acquaintance," and "It's lovely weather today." But she has apparently been thinking about her meeting with Truffaut for the whole plane ride to Mobile, and as I usher her to baggage she tells me she wants me to teach her a new introductory phrase. Something simple like, "Your view of life has changed my view of life." I, of course, refuse. We arrive on location and I introduce Lynnie to Truffaut. Her "It's a pleasure to make your acquaintance," goes very smoothly, and Truffaut is terrific. He calls her "mademoiselle" and says a few charming words in English. Lynnie is so overwhelmed by both Truffaut and the language barrier that she drops her usual intelligent and direct manner; she stammers and blushes and practically curtsies. She spends the night kicking herself for acting like a fool. Dreyfuss tells her not to be upset. He's been working with Truffaut for months and he *still* feels like an idiot whenever he's around him.

It is almost dark and Spielberg and his crew are lighting the inside of the jet. About seventy-five extras have been sitting in the plane for an hour, which, because of the lights, is like an oven. I bring Lynnie over to watch the shooting, but there is nothing we can see from outside the plane, so we go to the honeywagons and wait. Truffaut has been looking for a title for the book he is writing about acting, and he is thinking of calling it Hurry Up and Wait, which I think would be very apt. Especially tonight. It gets to be midnight and I still have not worked.

It's a hot, sticky night. I keep thinking I see rats under the trailer. They turn out to be giant palmetto bugs. The noise from the plane as it continuously backs up and taxis into position for the shot is deafening. A horrible night.

We break for dinner, get our food and take it to tables set up in an abandoned airplane hangar. I'm too uncomfortable to eat. After dinner we go back to the dressing room again, and I try to take a nap. As soon as I'm asleep, JB, the second assistant director, says we're ready to work. I knew the only way we'd ever get started was if I went to sleep.

Spielberg describes a brief scene he will shoot with me and an FBI agent.* We're supposed to be anxiously awaiting Truffaut's arrival, and I make a few comments about what a difficult guy I've heard he is: "He's gone through five interpreters in the last six months." We rehearse, but the man I'm doing the scene with has never acted before. He really *is* an FBI man, and he proclaims his lines in a very loud, clipped voice. Spielberg keeps reminding him that we are alone on a deserted runway and we are supposed to be speaking softly. Finally we get a good take.

Spielberg leads Truffaut and Lance and me over to a Cadillac limousine. He puts Lance in the driver's seat and Truffaut and me in the back seat and tells us to rehearse the scene. Truffaut is to give me a copy of a dirty book and have me translate a couple of pages into English:* "Her firm young breasts heaved with excitement as she slipped off her wooly sweater. Her nipples were as hard, pink and round as bubblegum." We all laugh. My character is supposed to be embarrassed. Spielberg tells me to practically yell the lines. Spielberg is right — it definitely is more embarrassing to translate porn at the top of my lungs.

We get to the end of the scene and Truffaut is supposed to ask Lance how I was. Lance's line is "Hot Damn", which Spielberg wants me to repeat to Truffaut in French. Truffaut and I go into a huddle and come up with an equivalent expression, "Du Tonnerre" — "Thunder and Lightning!" We ran through the scene once more, and miraculously we all seem to remember our lines. Spielberg is pleased because the scene is four or five pages long, and he would like to film it in one take, which means no line flubbing.

I wonder how we'll do when the car is really moving, and the airplane is actually taxiing around behind us, but I figure we've got all night. We may need it.

We rehearse once for camera positions. Lance is to start driving the limousine from a spot about two hundred feet in back of where I am standing. As he drives, a 707 jet taxis in an arc behind him, and by the time Lance hits his final position near the camera, the plane is to be framed in the rear window of the limousine. I'm not sure this could be done by Mario Andretti. We rehearse a few times. Lance turns out to be a terrific driver, and manages to hit his mark almost perfectly every time. Spielberg says we are going for a take. I'm sleepy and a little bored from all the hours of waiting, but I become surprisingly alert, and remember we are here to be in a movie, not just to wait around and have dinner in airplane hangars.

Lance pulls the car around in a perfect arc and the plane begins taxiing. The limo halts at exactly the right place, and the scene begins. I stick my head in the window and say hello to Truffaut. He lets me in the car and we introduce ourselves. It's going beautifully. We get to the part about the breasts. The plane is making a lot of noise, and I really do have to shout, and it seems good. Finally Lance says "Hot Damn", and I turn to Truffaut and say "Du Tonnerre" and Truffaut has a great expression on his face. We finish the scene, Spielberg yells, "Drive off, Lance!" and we lurch forward out of frame. The take was wonderful, and the crew applauds. They probably think they are going home early. Spielberg checks our end position through the camera and calls everyone back. The airplane wasn't visible through the limo window, and we have to do it again.

The next time the airplane's in the right place, but the car hits the wrong mark. And then I blow a line. As dawn is breaking, everybody finally gets everything right, and we leave for the hotel. We have to sleep all day because we're shooting again tonight. And the night after that. Welcome to Mobile, Lynnie.


## JULY 3

It's the Fourth of July weekend. The local Ku Klux Klan have been given permission to march in the Mobile Bicentennial Parade, provided they don't wear hoods. Being Mrs. Dreyfuss' son, as he puts it, Richard could not let this event pass without comment, and he has released a statement to the Associated Press saying that if the Klan has a right to march, he has a right to protest their existence. And he is protesting it vehemently.

Later that day, Richard receives a death threat. Julia assigns two bodyguards to Richard who follow him everywhere. They're burly, redneck types who look like they could have easily sent the threat themselves.

---

Tonight we're working in a deserted complex of buildings, doing a scene in which François and I interrogate Dreyfuss. We filmed us entering the room two months ago in Wyoming. It's a crucial scene, and Steven has re-written it a number of times. He has the newest version of the scene with him and has driven to work with us to go over it. We're trying to remember our new lines, and Steven is having trouble helping us because he has written them on a crumpled piece of paper and they're almost illegible. Since I haven't received a copy of the scene in advance, I haven't been able to translate it into French, and can't learn the dialogue. I have an AD bring me a large piece of cardboard and start madly scribbling French speeches on it. François' only English line tonight is a line from a previous draft which he's had under his belt for months, "Go outside and make a liar out of me."

We all go into the building where we'll be filming. A small office set has been constructed, and technicians are arranging lights as Steven shows us how we'll enter and sit. It's already ten o'clock, and I figure we won't actually shoot until after midnight. I ask why we're doing this scene at night since it takes place during the day, and Clark Paylow tells me that since we filmed last night and twelve hours is required between calls, we would have had to lose a whole day to shoot the scene in daylight. So here we are in Mobile at midnight, pretending it's noon in Wyoming, completing a scene we started in May.

I have trouble placing my cue card so it's not in the way of a light. We rehearse our entrance a couple of times. I am to enter briskly, sit down and turn on a tape recorder. We begin a take. I march into the room very efficiently, sit down with François and try to start the tape recorder. I can't find the 'Record' button. We march back to starting positions. The next take, everything goes really smoothly. François and I sit, I start the recorder, and we begin the scene. I have been filming for months, but this is the first scene I've filmed where I actually get to sit down and talk to someone. It feels good. Everyone is gathered around us listening intently to the scene. "It's like a real movie," I say to myself. The fact that we've just memorized it seems to be adding a nice feeling of spontaneity, and as François and I begin peppering Richard with questions, I'm aware that Julia Phillips and some casual observers are practically leaning in to listen to us. "Have you had migraines, trouble with your vision?" I continue questioning. Finally, I ask if Richard has had a close encounter. It's the first and only time the phrase is mentioned in the movie and I get to say it. You can hear a pin drop. The tension is enormous. François and I lean back and whisper for a moment, and finally Richard gets out of his chair and screams, "Who are you people?" Steven yells "Cut! Print!" and everyone runs over to congratulate us. It's like opening night. We film the scene from a lot of different angles, and then wait outside for a few minutes, so we can reverse directions.

We lean against the building and talk. Richard's guards are hovering nearby. It's past midnight and it's very deserted. We talk about how frightened Richard must be about his death threat, even with his guards. Then suddenly I realize people have been mistaking me for Dreyfuss ever since filming began. They don't know he doesn't have a beard or rimless glasses anymore. They would probably think I was Dreyfuss like everybody else in Mobile does. I'm very worried: I remind a production staffer that everyone thinks *I'm* Dreyfuss, and *my* life may be in danger, too. She rolls her eyes and acts very annoyed, "I suppose this means *you'll* want a bodyguard too." I feel very replaceable. Since I have a few days off I decide to fly with Lynnie back to New York and sit out this Fourth of July in safety.

## JULY 6

Back in Mobile. Today I met Phil Dodds, a studious-looking man who will play the part of Jean Claude, the man who plays the ARP console, and communicates with the Mothership through music. He is carrying a briefcase and a lot of books under his arm. I spot *The Foundation Trilogy*, and some electronics textbooks. I ask him what an ARP is. He says an ARP is a little like a Moog and an electronic piano. It has a keyboard, but by pulling a lot of dials and switches, the machine can make any sound imaginable, since the sound is produced by electronic circuits, not by reeds or strings or anything like that. Dodds works for ARP as a regional representative. He says that when he was in Mobile installing the ARP on the Big Set, Spielberg noticed him fooling around with it. He said Spielberg liked the way he looked and was impressed with how he handled the machine and asked him if he would like to be in the movie. Dodds said "Sure", and now here he is. He says he can't wait to get home because he really misses his baby daughter, and he has promised his boss that he would be back in two weeks, since it's the busy season. I do not think he will be back in two weeks. I keep my mouth shut.

## JULY 9

We're on the Big Set again. It's so hot today that the plastic on the sides of the modules is bubbling and peeling off. Tomorrow Spielberg begins shooting from the floor, and at last our faces will be visible. Up until now the cameras have been so far away we haven't even been recording dialogue. Assistant directors are running around with Polaroid pictures they took last week, making sure everyone is in their old positions so the shots will match. Truffaut, Lance and I are having trouble remembering where we ran to when we escaped the large flying object last Tuesday, and an AD is trying to locate the corresponding Polaroid shot. Finally, with great authority, he places us several feet in front of a module, and reminds us to duck when Spielberg calls action.

We confess that these last weeks have been a blur. We can barely remember having been here, let alone where we were standing. Someone gives the signal for the fog machines and we take our positions. Technicians wearing gas masks turn on their foggers and go about the set spreading clouds of smoke everywhere. We wait until there is just the right amount of fog for the shot. I keep asking if the fog is poisonous. I'm told it is absolutely safe, but why then, I wonder, are the foggers wearing gas masks?

We finish the shot quickly, and Spielberg comes down to talk to us. He explains that we will be shooting the next week totally out of sequence, and that in order to follow what is going on we will have to study the storyboards that he has posted outside the set. We'll begin with shots establishing our preparations for the Mothership's arrival. Then we'll shoot the light show from the Mothership. Strange objects and lights will be flying all around us, only we won't actually be seeing anything. The special effects crew will be putting in the UFOs in post-production. Spielberg takes out some color renderings of the effects to give us an idea of what we'll be pretending to see. If the special effects wind up looking anything like the drawings, they'll be spectacular.

Spielberg takes us aside to coach us. He tells me to begin the sequence tentatively, and build to an emotional climax by the time the Mothership leaves. He says my character is a very cool type who becomes totally overwhelmed by what's going on, and eventually gives in to all of his feelings. I like the idea. There's almost no dialogue for the next fifteen days, and without Spielberg's suggestions I would have felt completely at sea. He tells Lance that he is to become more and more paranoid as the sequence progresses, until he is practically out of his mind. He tells Truffaut to continue to be enchanted by everything that is going on. He says it's very important that Truffaut seem warm and friendly during the sequence. The audience's reactions to the extraterrestrials will be largely determined by Truffaut's reactions. He wants Truffaut to think of the extraterrestrials as little children. He knows how Truffaut likes little children.

---

Steven has been receiving reports of a guy who is running around L.A. pretending to be him. He's been getting people to pay for his dinners, and has been giving Steven a generally bad name. Steven is upset, so he takes an ad in *The Hollywood Reporter*. "To the gullible and defenseless: The man walking the streets of Los Angeles is not Steven Spielberg. Steven Spielberg is in Alabama, making *Close Encounters of the Third Kind*. At least do not allow this sad fraud to make you pay for dinner. This year, Steven Spielberg *can* afford a meal."

---

Some of the modules have television sets in them. Fast Eddie, a videotape expert, has to make sure that there are a constant stream of images going across the screens. Mostly, Fast Eddie shows pictures he took of the exterior of the base camp in Gillette. I ask why he is called 'Fast Eddie', but no one seems to know.

---

Post Script: Last night after we wrapped, Fast Eddie gave a little party to show some of his private videotape collection. Now I know why he's called Fast Eddie.

## JULY 10

Another day on the Big Set. We are shooting over-the-shoulder angles on people coming out of modules. Norman Dreyfuss is among a group of technicians who have to keep running out and looking up at the sky. It's really hot in the modules today, and they do endless takes. After about half an hour, I don't see Norman. He is sitting in a cool spot behind the module reading yesterday's stock market reports.

Truffaut and I are getting things down to a routine. A few jokes, maybe a pun or two, and then some kidding about his accent. Today whenever anybody says hello to him he says, "I am just a little frog," e.g., "Hi, François. How are you today?" Truffaut: "I yam joost a leetle frog."

Joe Hooker comes over and does his "Mozambique" bit, and I tell Truffaut a joke: a doctor comes into a hospital room to cheer up his patient: "I have good news and bad news. First the bad news: we've had to amputate both your legs. Now the good news: the patient in the next bed wants to buy your slippers." I laugh uproariously. Truffaut doesn't get it. He looks at me eagerly, waiting for me to get to the punchline. It's very hard to translate funny.

Dreyfuss keeps forgetting his security badge and gets kicked off the set. It's very embarrassing for the guards.

There is an extra in a wheelchair. I have assumed he is crippled, but I find out today the chair is a prop. When the Mothership lands next week this man will wheel his chair over to it, get caught in its gravitational field and fly through the air free of his chair.* I hear this and run over to Steven, to tell him a great idea: I should fly, too. My briefcase will get caught in the gravitational field, and I will go chasing after it and end up twenty feet in the air. Steven looks at me like I'm crazy. I tell him how I've been dying to fly since I was a child, and at the age of four had to be forcibly restrained from jumping out of open windows. Spielberg tells me he'll think about it. But I shouldn't get my hopes up.

## JULY 12

François tells me today that before he began work on *Close Encounters* he called up Jeanne Moreau for advice on acting. She said he wouldn't have any problems, but that smiling would be difficult. Truffaut says her observation has been accurate. He also says that whenever he worked with Moreau she would develop a passionate hate for someone around the set: another actor, a wardrobe person, anyone. She would become fixated on this person. Days would become an endless series of avoided looks, delayed confrontations and hidden anger. Moreau explained that it did not have much to do with anything the other person was doing, it's just that when you're working for a long time in the same place, a scapegoat relieves the boredom and is good for concentration. Truffaut tells me he is choosing a scapegoat himself. I tell him I am, too. We don't tell each other who they are; we'll see if we can guess later. I am very grateful I have Truffaut there to talk with all the time. I'm aware sometimes of other people looking enviously at us as we joke and laugh and tell each other great stories in French, and I feel very lucky and a little possessive.

---

George Lucas, an old friend of Steven's, has come to observe, and he and Steven sit together watching a rehearsal. Julia comes by to say hello and the staff photographers have a field day. Lucas is editing a science fiction movie called *Star Wars.* Steven says that from what he's heard it should be very good.

---

This afternoon we are shooting Truffaut's reaction to a hovering UFO, touch it, and back away in awe. He rehearses this several times and then Steven shoots it. There is no dialogue, but it's hard to touch thin air and have a reaction of wonderment, happiness and awe at the same time. Steven has Truffaut do the scene over and over. I ask Truffaut if he minds a suggestion. He says of course not. I tell him that when he reaches up to touch the object he's got one hand on his hip and it looks too casual. I say that with his hand at his side he would probably look more reverential. Truffaut says "Aha!" and does the next take wonderfully, hand at his side. Spielberg yells "Print", and I'm proud of myself. Truffaut asks me to keep watching him closely. He's afraid that his friends will laugh at him when they see the film, but I tell him not to worry.

**JULY 13**

I haven't seen Norman Dreyfuss for a couple of days. Richard tells me he's left. He says he tried to tell his father how boring it is to make a movie, but he says no one really believes that — they think that it may be boring to *other* people, but *they* will find it glamorous and exciting. It's been four weeks since Norman arrived, but he couldn't stand the heat, and he couldn't stand the boredom, so he's gone back home. Funny, I always thought it was pretty hot and boring in Pasadena.

---

Truffaut sees me bringing my Bullworker Exerciser to the set today. A Bullworker is an exercise machine that, if used every day, would probably turn me into Steve Reeves. I can't seem to get around to using it every day. Truffaut wants to see how it works, and wonders if I know any good stomach exercises. He is very conscientious about being in shape, which I admire. I also admire how he thinks I am in shape enough to ask how to stay in shape. I promise to help him.

**JULY 14**

Went to Truffaut's room this morning. It's a suite, which at the Mobile Sheraton means it looks exactly like my tiny room, only there are two of them.

I have taken his request very seriously and have written down every stomach exercise I can think of. I demonstrate them for him one by one, pretending ease and trying to hide my gasps for air. Then he takes the Bullworker and goes through the exercises easily. He is in much better shape than I am.

We never mention exercises again.

---

**Miscellany:**

... It's getting hotter. The air-conditioning has to be turned off most of the time since we're recording sound, and when it's on full blast it doesn't really do too much good. François and I talk about our scapegoats. I am about to reveal my scapegoat, when my scapegoat comes over. François smiles and says hello, and then tells me what a wonderful person my scapegoat is. I don't have the guts to confess. Very frustrating.

... François is very up on current events. Every day we talk about some new atrocity Idi Amin has committed. Today he's finishing *The Final Days*, which is one of his favorite books.

---

... The fog machines are making especially thick fog today. I have now learned that the fog has a mineral oil base. It's a wonder we haven't been laxatived to death.

---

... I realize in the middle of the afternoon that I have no idea what we are filming today. I ask François and he doesn't really know either. We are supposed to be watching something in the sky, but no one seems to remember what exactly. The extra who has been dubbed "Dr. Einstein" comes over to me. He's called this because he has very long grey hair that is teased out at the ends, and he wears his tie thrown over his shoulder. He devised this outfit on the first day of shooting and has had to dress in the exact same ridiculous manner ever since. I ask Dr. Einstein what he does. He is a scientist. He tells me he's on vacation from a local university, where he has spent the last seven years doing experiments on rats, trying to isolate the chemical that causes aging. So far he has been totally unsuccessful. I don't wonder.

---

... Another extra, who hasn't spoken to me since we started shooting, comes over to me and asks if he can give me something. I say, "Sure," and shyly he hands me three pen and ink drawings of very bizarre-looking flying saucers. He wants me to have them. I put them in my briefcase and then look up as I notice the ARP being pulled forward, and someone making an announcement. Julia Phillips pushes in a huge sheet cake, and someone turns on the fan next to the French flag. Phil starts playing the 'Marseillaise' on the ARP. We all stand up and make François come forward and take a bow. It's Bastille Day. I still can't remember what scene we're shooting today, but I'm having a very good time.

## JULY 16

The days on the Big Set are becoming almost indistinguishable. We all refer to this sequence as the ―― Sequence. (During the ―― Sequence we look up at the sky and follow an imaginary UFO from right to left).

Today is different. As we are filming a shot in which Truffaut and I and the three hundred extras are running away from a small UFO, a semi-hurricane north wind comes up. A small pin-hole of light appears at the back of the tarp. As the wind gets stronger, the hole gets bigger and bigger. Then with a great tearing sound the tarp splits, and the wind flaps it around wildly, like a giant flag, until finally, the tarpaulin just rips off the hangar. The rear portion of the set is totally exposed. The sky looks like it's cut in two — one side giant black thunderheads, and the other brilliant white clouds. Then the sky turns yellow and sheets of rain come pouring into the Big Set. People freeze for a moment, regarding the awesome spectacle, then spring into action, trying to salvage the tarp. Truffaut holds his fingers to his face to frame the scene, and watches motionless for several minutes as the crew tries to fasten down what's left of the tarpaulin. Later he says he hopes Spielberg has kept the cameras rolling; visually, this is the most exciting thing he's seen since we've started filming.

## JULY 17

We have to stop filming on the Big Set for a few days until the tarp is repaired, so Richard and Teri film the scene in front of their house where Neary grabs the wire fencing from the duck pen and starts throwing things through his window to build the mock-up of Devil's Tower.

It's very hot and they've been working long hours and Richard has taken a giant load of dirt and mistakenly hurled it at Vilmos Zsigmond, the cinematographer, and the camera. No one can stop laughing for five minutes, and everybody's talking about it tonight. "Did you hear? Richard threw the dirt at Vilmos! Ha! Ha! Ha! Ha! Ha!" The heat is finally getting to us.

Teri says she was walking in the woods around the house, between takes, and was chased out by the wildlife. She says the whole area is covered with frogs and armadillos.

There was trouble with the ducks today. When Richard removed their fence they were supposed to escape, but every time he pulled it up, they just sat there quietly. They wouldn't scatter. Finally Spielberg did a take without sound, and got the ducks to move by yelling at them.

**Miscellany:**

... It took Joe and his crew almost a week to build the mountain that Neary builds in his living room. It's made of styrofoam, and covered with plaster, and there was a big controversy over how professional-looking to make it. Spielberg wanted to make sure that when you saw the Tower on TV, there was no question Richard's model was the same thing. The model is an exact replica of the Tower, complete with little trees, and a notch at the top. It's perfect, except for one thing — they built it too big to get it through the front door of the house. They have to cut the Tower in half, bring it into the house, and stick it back together again.

---

**JULY 19**

I almost overslept this morning. The driver had to ring my room and wake me up. I rushed like crazy, and we managed to get to the hangar at the usual 7 A.M. It's a madhouse. Spielberg has announced the Mothership is finally ready to land, and hundreds of extras, ETs, and mimes are milling around waiting to work.

When the giant ship lands, the ETs will make their long-awaited arrival. After the ETs arrive, we will film the "returnees" leaving the ship. World War II fighter pilots missing in action will return unharmed. A Judge Crater lookalike will return, as well as the entire crew of Flight 19 that disappeared in the Bermuda Triangle.

There's a feeling of excitement in the air. Relatives of Steven's and Richard's have come to Mobile for the occasion, and they mill around watching the frenzied preparation. ETs have skid-proof pads attached to the bottoms of their leotards. The Amelia Earhart lookalike is sick, and a new lookalike is frantically getting pinned into her costume.

The ship took longer than expected to be completed and the picture is several million dollars over budget. Rumors of angry Columbia executives are mounting. The other day I saw a group of Iranian businessmen in the lobby of the hotel and somebody said they were here to be wooed as potential backers of the film.

Spielberg has been making changes in the ET heads up to the very last minute. Yesterday, some new heads arrived for use in closeups. They have eyes that move by radio control, and children strong enough to support these heavier heads are being recruited. An old batch of overly threatening-looking heads is piled outside the makeup room waiting to be returned to

Los Angeles. I finish in makeup and hurry into the Big Set.

The Mothership is perched in the middle of the landing strip looking unbelievably huge and extremely eerie. Steven keeps explaining that what we see is only the tiniest part of the bottom of the ship, and tries to give us an idea of how big it will actually look. It's hard for me to grasp the ultimate size of this thing. A giant crane is raising and lowering the Mothership in preparation for the scene, and the whole area is bathed in the glow of a terrifically bright light. Dozens of technicians are running around making final adjustments. The lighting crew is inside the ship focusing the arcs that will reflect off the ship's silver mylar interior. Stunt coordinators help the children into their heads and hands, and assistant directors arrange the extras in large clumps along the runway. Some of the ETs will fly,* and technicians are raising and lowering sandbags, and realigning pulley systems that stretch across the set. They anticipate problems with the flying.

Steven wants the entire scene heavily backlit, and this may make the wires show up too much. No one will know how the scene has gone until it's viewed in dailies tomorrow. Some of the ETs are practicing entering and exiting the ship. The rumor that they were to originally glide out on concealed rollerskates was true, but the exit ramp from the ship is too steep, and now they are rehearsing sitting down and sliding out of the ship. Once they make it up the ramp they slide down easily, but many of them can only make it halfway up before they slip back to the bottom, and stunt people are stationed along the ship pulling the kids up, and helping them as they glide down. Susan is giving them some last minute instructions, and reminds them to use "loving" hand gestures.

François and I go over to talk to one of the little girls. As we talk to her, she slowly rises a few feet off the ground. We hadn't noticed the wire attached to her waist; François is enchanted. We look around and see seven or eight more little ETs bouncing around five, ten, even twenty feet up in the air. It's magical. One little girl hangs motionless, high above us, while a technician adjusts her pulley. She notices us watching and starts to flap her arms. The unruly kids of three weeks ago are now acting calmer and more professionally than the rest of us.

After much rehearsal and positioning, the ETs are loaded into the Mothership which slowly rises about fifteen feet. The heat building up inside the ship is tremendous, and Spielberg says we must hurry and film or the kids will get baked. He yells "action" and four cameras begin to roll simultaneously. The spaceship sinks slowly to the ground. The bottom slides open. A blinding light streams out of the ship, enveloping us as we stand transfixed. A large ramp appears in the sulphurous fog and spindly ETs start tentatively crawling out of the ship, gliding and rolling down the ramp which bridges the concrete Wyoming landing strip with another universe. Suddenly, nine or ten ETs fly out of the ship, twirl around, wave their arms and swoop over our heads. One or two hover near the ship, turning endless somersaults. Mimes dressed as technicians move about the ETs in slow motion. A creature comes forward, haltingly. Then it breaks into a disco hustle. "Cut", yells Spielberg, to the rubber-suited children. "ETs, stop fooling around!"

The Mothership has landed.

Everyone goes back to their original marks and we do the scene over and over. We're all getting a little punchy, especially the kids, who have been flying and crawling for several hours, almost non-stop. After twenty minutes of re-lighting and preparing the fog effect we're about to begin a take, when three of the ETs have to go to the bathroom. No one ever thought to put a trap door in their costumes, and it takes them each a full ten minutes to get into and out of their skin tight leotards. So we wait for the kids, and pray that by the time they get back three more don't have to go.

In the middle of a take, one of the ETs pulls off another one's rubber hand and starts batting her over the head with it. A fight breaks out. Steven decides we're finished for the day and we all go over to the kids to congratulate them. They've been generally terrific, and have been able to follow direction much better than anyone thought they would. They take off their heads and hands, pick up their coloring books and trudge off to their dressing room to get into their street clothes. They look like they've been doing this for twenty years.

## JULY 20

At the pool today Truffaut asks me if I wouldn't mind reading a script for him. He reads English very well, but someone has sent him a sci-fi script, and he is having trouble understanding some of the technical terms. I am tremendously flattered and run up to my room to read it immediately.

It's not a very good script, but I read it thoroughly and take copious notes; I want to give Truffaut an accurate report. Later he asks me what I thought. I fill him in on the story. I launch into an incredibly boring scene-by-scene synopsis. Truffaut listens very politely as I ramble on for fifteen minutes, re-telling every trivial incident in the complicated script. I give possible meanings and interpretations for every twist and turn of its convoluted plot. I am trying much too hard. Finally he stops me. He smiles: "Could you please just tell me if you think it's good or bad?"

I go to Steven's house tonight to see a movie. He's screening *Battleground*. Almost all of its exteriors were shot in the studio; almost all of our exteriors are being shot in the studio, so I guess that's why he wants to watch the film. Steven screens a movie almost every night, and his taste is eclectic. Last night it was *The Canterville Ghost*. I drive to the house with two guys who have come to Mobile to do some work with Steven on their screenplay, which he may direct. Their names are Bob Zemeckis and Bob Gale. I never can remember which is which, so I just call them The Two Bobs. So does everyone else. They are always together so this is no problem. If I ran into one of them alone I guess I'd have to call him The One Bob, but this has never happened. Their script, about a Japanese attack on L.A., is wonderful. They go about retelling parts of their screenplay for Steven, each taking different parts and acting out the scenes together. They have been here for almost two weeks and have spent maybe four hours with Steven. They are getting desperate.

We pull up to the rear of Spielberg's rented ranch house and enter through the enclosed porch. Steven has converted this into editing facilities. Mike Kahn, the editor, does most of his work in this room. We wend our way through the movieolas and a series of dog bowls and chew-sticks, trying not to step on Elmer, Steven's cocker spaniel. Elmer is wonderful. He is the silliest animal I have ever seen. He looks like Walt Disney made him up. He has a great shock of hair that stands up on his head like electrified pick-up sticks. He is very sweet. Steven got him during *Jaws* and Elmer used to spend a lot of time out on the boat with him.

We go through the kitchen and introduce ourselves to Steven's cook. She is making a lot of great-looking food and mumbling about how no one ever sits down to eat on time so the food is always cold. My mouth is watering. Mobile food is not terrific, and I haven't had a homecooked meal for a long time. I will personally see to it that everyone sits down while the food is still hot.

The dining room table is set and a projector sits beside it. We will watch the movie during dinner. Steven is in the hallway playing the organ. He loves to play the organ. He has never studied, but he spends hours picking out songs and inventing melodies. He can pick out the background music from all of his favorite movies, and he and Truffaut play a running game of "Guess what movie this song is from?" He rented this organ, and though it is very small it has a rhythm section which supposedly can sound like everything from a clarinet to a xylophone. It all sounds like an organ to me.

Steven tells me he has gotten the rights to the original recording of Ukelele Ike singing 'When You Wish Upon A Star' and is going to play the song in its entirety over the Mothership's departure.* I think this is a fabulous idea.

Steven plays the song on the organ as we all sing along in Jiminy Cricket's squeaky voice. When we get to the high note on "... no request is too extreme..." we break into a falsetto yelp that makes Elmer leave the room. I think it's a wonderful idea to end the movie with this sweet song. The Two Bobs think so too. Steven asks if we would like to hear the song on his stereo and takes out the full orchestration and plays it for us. We sit there imagining the end of the movie. I can see the ship taking off... Truffaut and I waving goodbye to the ETs... stars twinkling... My fantasy even includes a red velvet curtain coming down and wild applause at the final credits.

Dinner is ready, and I make everyone sit down immediately. The cook passes around some great-looking corned beef and cabbage and Rick Fields gets the projector ready. The Two Bobs tell funny stories about another idea they have for a movie. As one starts a joke the other winds up with the punchline, and before the laughter has died down they are doing variations. The projector begins to whir, and The Two Bobs are building on a hilarious situation involving a car salesman in Las Vegas. The titles start, everyone yells shush. The Two Bobs have to wait till the next reel change to continue their story.

The *Battleground* titles appear. Steven knows the credits of everybody in the cast. I enjoy the movie. The reel ends, The Two Bobs finish their Las Vegas story and the cook brings out dessert. I hope Steven invites me again because I'm having a very good time. The next reel comes up, and by now almost everyone has fallen asleep. By the time the last grenade is thrown, the only ones awake are me and Elmer.


## JULY 23

We're all beginning to get a little spooked. Last night some people thought they saw a UFO over the hangar. By the time Spielberg and the rest of us ran outside to look, the lights had disappeared.

Dr. J. Allen Hynek, a Northwestern University astronomy professor, and technical advisor to the movie, arrived today to make a brief appearance in the film as one of the returnees. He is wearing a Hawaiian shirt and doesn't look much like a scientist except for his neatly cropped Van Dyck beard which makes him look a little like the Wizard of Oz. He thinks the movie will help the UFO cause since Steven has done such thorough research, and based so much of the film on actual events. He says that the mailboxes and roadsigns shaking during Richard's car sequence are based on an actual report. He also says UFOs have stopped cars, and the burns that Richard and Melinda have on their hands and faces have been reported many times.

He tells me that there have been sightings of huge ships, like the Mothership, but says that there have never been reports of anything as large as the Mothership actually landing. No photographs can be taken on the set, so Hynek sits quietly in his canvas chair aiming a small tape recorder in the direction of the filming. Since he can't take pictures, he's taping the sounds in the hangar to help him remember this day.

Later that night, Hynek gives a lecture to us interested UFO-ers. Dreyfuss and Melinda are there, along with about forty other people. After a short spiel about subscribing to a UFO newsletter he's publishing, Hynek dims the lights and shows slides of various UFOs he's authenticated. He even shows a picture of an umbrella-like object he snapped from an airplane. About a dozen people, including Melinda, raise their hands when Hynek asks if any of us have ever had a close encounter. When Hynek leaves, we sit around telling stories about little UFOnauts who have been deep frozen in places like Albuquerque.

Dreyfuss reminds us about the recent stories in the paper about a couple from another planet who have been going around and getting families to leave their homes in preparation for an outer space flight. Dreyfuss feels we may be "racing the cosmos," and the filming better go quickly. He jokes we have to prevent whoever's out there from landing until the movie opens. I mention a rumor that the film is part of the necessary training that the human race must go through in order to accept an actual landing, and is being secretly sponsored by a government UFO agency. It's like ghost stories at camp.

I drive back to the hotel with Melinda and Merrill Connally. Merrill is the brother of former Texas Governor John Connally. He acted in *The Sugarland Express* before getting his role in *CE3K*, but he's not always an actor. He owns several thousand acres of grazing land in Texas, and was once LBJ's Texas campaign manager. He's 6' 6", has a great mane of silver hair, and is referred to as the American Eagle on the daily call sheets. When Merrill says something you believe him. Merrill says that both his wife and best friend have had close encounters of the second kind with UFOs (physical evidence), and he describes a flying saucer chase down a Texas road that has me looking over my shoulder as I go to my room.

## JULY 24

Truffaut gave me another script to read. The author wants him to direct it, and he wants to send a very quick reply. The author has enclosed an extremely emotional letter with his script, describing the depth of his feelings for the material and the trials he has been going through trying to get it produced. I tell Truffaut that unfortunately the script is very much like another movie that I've just seen, and is not very well written. I give Truffaut a brief synopsis of the plot. It's not something he would be interested in, but he admires the writer. He thinks hard for a moment; he wants to say something nice to the man. He gets an idea: he will write a letter explaining that the subject matter is too personal to be directed by anyone other than the author. He thanks me for reading it so quickly.

He goes to his desk and pulls out a book. It's the novel of his movie, *Small Change*. He writes a brief inscription on the inside cover and hands it to me. I can't stop smiling. I put the book away in my briefcase. For the rest of the day whenever I'm alone I take it out and look at the inscription:

> For Laughlin with my gratitude
> For Bob with my friendship
>
> François Truffaut
> July 76

## JULY 26

I don't have anything to do after lunch. The light crew is re-rigging some of the ceiling lights so Steven can film reflections from the UFOs. It's pretty deserted. I wander down a corridor and hear kids laughing. I stick my head in a door and see Susan Heldfond attempting to teach her little ETs some new movements. Today they're throwing food. Susan is practically in tears. Down the hall, the staff artist is in his cubicle completing his thousandth rendering of the week. This one shows a pie-shaped wedge flying over some technicians. I look over his shoulder for a while. His earlier drawings had only faceless clusters of men surrounded by very detailed special effects, but this sketch contains a very French-looking man and a short person with a beard and glasses. The short person is carrying an attache case.

I wander into another room. Everyone yells, "Duck!" Steven is screening dailies. I watch the screen. The clapboard comes on: "CE3K. DIR: SPIELBERG. CAMERA: ZSIGMOND. INT. NGHT. SC. 183." I can see Melinda waiting nervously in the background. It's the scene where the UFO comes to her house and kidnaps Cary Guffey through the doggy door. She keeps clasping her hands to her mouth as she waits for the cracking of the sticks signalling the beginning of the scene. A strange orange light is glowing. I hear Spielberg's voice on the film: "OK, Melinda, that last one was terrific. Just remember we

need to see more of Cary's body this time. Don't block him with your hair."
Melinda gives a quick nod. The sticks crack.

The clapboard is removed and Melinda begins the scene. She turns towards the camera frantically. She is crying. She runs after Cary Guffey who is almost at the doggy door. The door is flapping, and every time it opens more orange light streams into the room. Smoke begins to creep under the window. The scene really looks scary, even without music and editing. Cary starts crawling out the door and Melinda hurls herself to the floor and grabs at his ankles. But something out there is pulling him through the door. Sweat pours from Melinda's forehead as she desperately pulls on Cary, and whatever is outside just keeps pulling harder. "Try harder, Melinda," Steven quietly urges from off-camera. Little Cary's body is being pulled in both directions like a piece of taffy. Melinda makes one last pull, and Cary comes flying back into the room. He lands on top of Melinda and the two of them start laughing uproariously. Steven chuckles off-camera. Whatever was outside was supposed to win; Melinda got carried away. Score one for the Earthlings.

---

**Miscellany:**

... I watch another scene where Cary comes down the stairs in his pjs to see what's going on. He notices something off-camera, laughs. I hear dialogue off-camera, like, "Cary, look over here," but I can't tell what the voice is referring to. Someone tells me later that Spielberg always has things for Cary to look at off-camera. When Cary came down the stairs that day, Steven had the makeup man dress up in a giant bear costume and wait to surprise Cary at the bottom of the stairs.

---

... When Barry (Cary) gets grabbed through the doggy door after the ET attack on the house, Jillian (Melinda) has to run outside to look for him. She's running outside of a real house, but looking up at a special effects sky. She must stay below the horizon line, because Doug Trumbull is putting special cloud effects and a light show over the real Mobile sky.

---

... Steven tells me he is filming this movie in 70-millimeter for a very specific reason. He says in most movies you can tell whenever the special effects are about to come on because just before they do, the quality of the film changes: it gets grainier and a little darker. This is the natural result of manipulating the image to produce the special effect, and it is impossible to avoid. He says you don't usually notice it consciously, but you become subliminally aware that a special effect is coming up, so you are prepared for it when it appears. He wants to avoid that in *CE3K*. He will film all special effects scenes in 70-millimeter and all the other scenes in 35-millimeter. When the film is put together, he will blow up the 35-millimeter to 70-millimeter. Blowing up the 35-millimeter causes it to get grainier. In the final print, the film quality of the non-special effects scenes will match the film quality of the special effects scenes, and the audience will be taken by total surprise when the effects appear. I think someone should give me an Honorary Degree for understanding this.

## JULY 27

I'm having breakfast at the Sheraton Inn coffee shop with a Mobile city official. The steam tables are set up for the $3.99 Weekend Brunch Special, and the smell of Sterno is overpowering. The official says he appreciates the employment the movie has generated in Mobile, and I ask him a few tourists' questions, like what to see in Mobile, and did Sandy Koufax really have a bunk in the USS Alabama. Then I ask him if he's ever seen a UFO. He doesn't look like the type who'd admit it even if he had, so I'm surprised to learn the following: in the early fifties, he was stationed on a radar unit in the Far East. He often tracked unscheduled aircraft flying over Japan on his scanner, and would send planes out to follow. The aircraft would change directions and disappear at unheard-of speeds. This was fairly common, he explains. Everyone was pretty used to it. In fact, they eventually stopped reporting the incidents.

I ask him what everyone thought they were seeing, zipping around up there. And he tells me very matter-of-factly that everyone generally felt they were seeing a spaceship. I try hard not to look amazed, but I am. I can't wait to relay this information to Dr. Hynek, who is always on the lookout for respectable people who have seen UFOs.

---

We're filming "cuboids" today, the small white, brightly lit boxes that will come streaming out of the Mothership and form long, winding rows that dance over our heads and all around the Big Set.*

I noticed technicians building the cuboids the other day. They were stringing 5" square boxes made of plywood and rice paper on to miles of electrical wire. Each box has a 500-watt bulb inside. I can see at least thirty or forty boxes strung up already, and a lot more in the corner.

We're being positioned next to the cuboids, which are lined up, unlighted, on the floor about ten feet in front of us. We are warned not to go anywhere near the wires that will support the cuboids, and never to touch an actual cuboid as it whizzes by our faces, as there will be about 20,000 volts of electricity streaming through them and we will get fried. This is the first time we will actually witness a special effect as it is taking place.

The filming today will be intercut with long shots of the cuboids that will be put in later. We wait a long time for the cuboids to get properly strung up. They're heavy, and the wire that supports them is drooping. Finally, everything is ready, and Steven turns on the power for a rehearsal. The amount of light generated by these little boxes is blinding and will, hopefully, flare out and hide the support wires. Steven has Vilmos over-expose the scene for protection. The cuboids are arranged on pulleys that move back and forth like a laundry washline. As the pulley is operated and the cuboids move in front of us, we watch carefully, making sure not to get anywhere near the highly charged little boxes. I can see the headline now: "Actors Killed in Mobile by Falling Cuboids."

Nick McLean is over in a corner of the set working with the computerized camera. When Steven yells action, Nick turns on the camera and the camera travels, all by itself, down metal track-guides, panning right to left. It is guided by a closet-sized computer that makes a continuous record of its velocity and direction for the special effects matte artists in Doug Trumbull's Hollywood office. As the camera shuttles along, we gather around and smile encouragingly, as if the camera were an actor on his first day of work.

(Continued on page 113.)

# WYOMING

Filming began on May 16, 1976 at Devil's Tower near Gillette, Wyoming. We shot for two weeks but it felt more like two months. Days we filmed Dreyfuss and Melinda's approach to the base camp at the foot of Devil's Tower, and exterior sequences with Truffaut and me. Everyday at twilight Dreyfuss and Melinda filmed their chase up the tower. Mornings we made the two-hour drive from the hotel trying to stay awake, and evenings we drove home, hoping our drivers wouldn't run into one of the deer which filled the roads. We hated the food, and the main entertainment at location was a prairie dog town, but we didn't realize how much we'd miss the cool, dry weather once we got to Mobile.

Truffaut and I in our first days of shooting. I act up a storm, and then realize I cannot be seen, since my breath has fogged my gas mask.

Truffaut and I are hundreds of feet up in the helicopter when suddenly the door opens, and we almost fall out. We have to film the remainder of the scene clutching our seat belts and holding the door shut.

Truffaut and I try to convince Warren Kemmerling (left) to allow Richard to stay on the mountain. Spielberg loved Truffaut in this scene, but wanted to subtitle his dialogue in English. It turned out Truffaut *was* speaking English!

If Steven Spielberg (center, with bullhorn) looks a little tense, it's because we've just shot a scene where Richard's car hurtled through a barbed wire fence, and one of the camera crew got caught in the barbed wire. Fortunately, he wasn't hurt. We all stepped back twenty feet on the next take.

No matter what else we were doing, everyday at dusk we had to stop and shoot Richard, Melinda and Joe Sommers running up the mountain. Steven had to make sure that their escape was filmed in the same light he had used in the previous footage.

Spielberg (right) asks Truffaut, Lance Henriksen (center right) and I to improvise a scene about flying to the other side of the Tower. I tell Truffaut to bring an extra scarf in case it gets cold, but I forget the French word for scarf, and end up telling him to bring an extra tie.

Melinda and Dreyfuss filmed this evacuation scene in Bay Minette, Alabama but were supposedly in Wyoming near Devil's Tower. It's 110 degrees outside and Melinda's boxcar is jammed with hundreds of extras and it's even hotter in there. This scene made work on the Big Set look easy.

Dreyfuss, Melinda and Joe Sommers are escaping, running past the building where Truffaut and I are trying to convince Warren Kemmerling to let the trio stay and watch the Mothership land. Truffaut had to watch them run by from the window and then turn back to the window smiling, but since Melinda's ankle was sprained she couldn't reach her final mark by the time Truffaut was supposed to notice her. It took almost a dozen takes to get this one.

The Major Walsh scene. Truffaut and I try to convince Warren Kemmerling to let Dreyfuss stay and greet the Mothership. Truffaut has pasted cue cards around the room with his English dialogue on it. He's even got one on Major Walsh's chest!

# MOBILE
## (OFF THE BIG SET)

When we weren't filming on the Big Set, we filmed on location in and around Mobile. Truffaut and I met at the Mobile airport in a scene that was eventually cut from the movie, and Melinda and Cary spent days being chased around by UFOs and weird orange lights in a house just outside the city. The motel where Melinda saw Devil's Tower on T.V. was built here, and Dreyfuss had his 'close encounter' with the UFO on a Mobile back road. The Crescendo Summit Set was constructed next to the hangar that housed the Big Set. Poor Richard and Melinda and Teri spent weeks waiting for something to go wrong with the Big Set so they could film one of their sequences.

Spielberg is directing Truffaut in the scene at the Holiday Inn. He's about to tell him to look up at the sky in anticipation of the eventual arrival of the Mothership, and it's the first look to the sky Spielberg has filmed. It's a very exciting moment for everyone. At one point Spielberg called the picture 'Watch the Skies'.

In this well-known shot of Dreyfuss looking at the UFO for the first time, the bright lights giving him the 'space burn' are really giant movie arc lights suspended above the truck.

Cary Guffey is watching these objects with the exact expression of wonderment that Spielberg wanted. Cary seemed to be able to do whatever Spielberg wanted and had absolutely no self-consciousness in front of the camera. During the filming he and Spielberg had an almost uncanny ability to communicate with each other.

In this shot, Cary Guffey comes downstairs in his pajamas and sees the UFOs for the first time. To get that wondrous expression on Cary's face, Steven Spielberg had one of the crew dress up in a bear suit and surprise Cary when he came down the stairs.

This idyllic picnic knoll on Crescendo Summit is really a set built in the Mobile hangar adjoining the Big Set. There were real trees and grass on the Summit, and while on most movie sets the greenery dies almost immediately, the greenery here thrived on the humidity of the stifling summer weather.

This is Crescendo Summit. It's the first time we see UFO special effects in the movie. And in post-production when Richard Dreyfuss saw this effect for the first time, he was so excited he almost fell out of his chair.

When Steven Spielberg viewed the scenes where Cary is taken by the UFO, he decided they weren't scary enough. So he went back and added shots post-production of the UFOs trying to get in through the floor grating, including the terrifying shots of the screws turning.

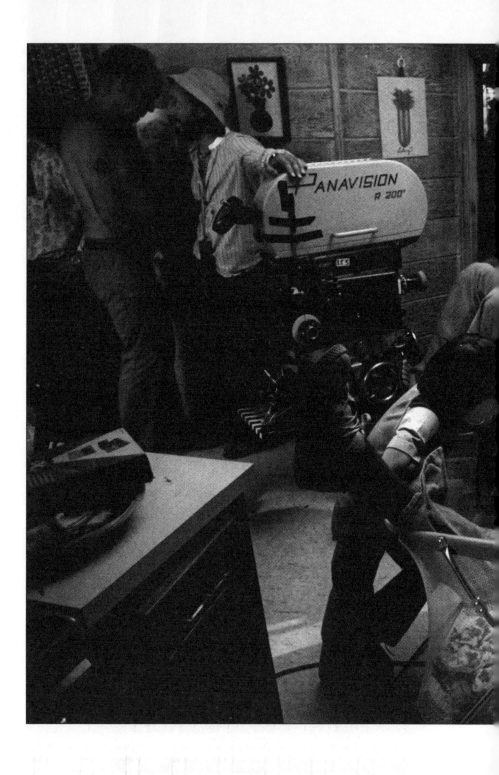

Spielberg is kidding around with Dreyfuss' nephew, Justin, between takes. He always wanted Justin to play Richard's son, since there's such a strong family resemblance, but Justin wanted to spend the summer playing baseball and had to be convinced he'd have just as much fun being in a movie. Looks like Spielberg's trying to make good on his promise.

The Neary family is in their den being directed by Spielberg. They've had to cut one of the walls of the house out to accommodate all of the equipment necessary for filming. Columbia decided to buy the house, since they were to put in so many improvements, and after filming sold it at a profit.

Dreyfuss is building his miniature Devil's Tower. You'll notice you can't see the time on his wristwatch. He's wearing a digital watch — a neat way of solving continuity problems.

Dreyfuss is stealing the fencing from the lady next door's duck pen. Spielberg had no trouble directing the human actors in this scene, but couldn't get the ducks to move at the right moment. Finally he filmed a take without sound and had someone yell at the ducks when it was time for them to scatter.

Neary was trying to get his wife not to leave him here, but the idea of not having to film any more in this bug-infested, crowded, incredibly hot location must have been making him secretly very happy.

Dreyfuss is hurling refuse into his house to create the indoor Devil's Tower. Everybody's getting a little punchy from the heat and long hours and in one take Dreyfuss hurls a load of dirt right at the camera. Filming has to be curtailed long enough for everyone to stop laughing.

This is the scene where Melinda has to recognize Devil's Tower on the News. Since she is supposed to have traveled to New Mexico searching for her son, Joe Alves had to build a tacky pseudo-Western motel room, in an adjoining hangar in the complex. If Melinda looks a little bleary-eyed, it could be because this scene was shot at 8 A.M.

Dreyfuss is completing his Devil's Tower. The real one is about to appear on T.V. There was a raging controversy as to how realistic Richard's creation should be, and it was finally decided to make it very realistic. Spielberg wanted instant recognition when the Tower appeared on T.V.

In the auditorium scene where he teaches us the Kodaly hand signals, Truffaut had extensive English dialogue. He was very nervous about this scene, and rehearsed and rehearsed it. Finally, he was letter perfect, *except* he forgot how to pronounce one word — "something".

Spielberg is directing us in the scene in which we finally ask if Dreyfuss has had a 'Close Encounter'. Dreyfuss has received a death threat, and his two bodyguards are standing somewhere off to the left. Everyone has been mistaking me for Dreyfuss so my life may be in more danger than his.

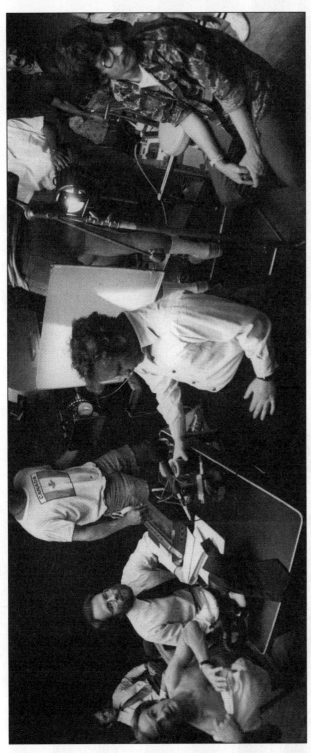

It's so hot in our tiny set we have to keep changing our shirts which are drenched with sweat. Steven never put this scene in the screenplay — he handed us our lines on pieces of paper, and we learned them on the spot.

Truffaut and I are trying to convince Warren Kemmerling to let Dreyfuss into the mountain. Dreyfuss uses this opportunity to sneak past the guards and onto the landing area.

# THE BIG SET

Columbia built the Big Set in a huge airplane hangar in Mobile, Alabama after investigating everything from the Goodyear Blimp hangar to the Houston Astrodome. It was almost impossible to air-condition. We spent months of fourteen-hour days here trying in vain to keep cool. Every morning the actors would present their security badges to the guards in front, go to makeup, and join the 400 extras for more days of looking up at the ceiling and pretending to see things. (Almost all of the special effects were put in post-production.) An artist in one of the offices upstairs spent his days doing renderings of shots that were about to be filmed. For this sequence of the Mothership landing we referred to pictures rather than a script to let us know what we were filming. An occasional hurricane would blow off the tarpaulin on the hangar extension making shooting impossible.

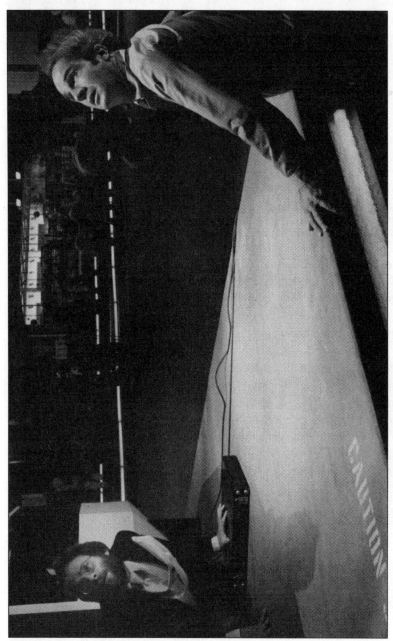

Truffaut and I are pretending to watch a flying object pass over us. Hidden air ducts are blowing our hair and our clothing, and lights hung from a large tram circle over our heads to simulate the effect of the UFO which will be added later in post-production.

Spielberg has cast Merrill Connally, the former Texas governor's brother, in the role of the team leader. He's referred to as the "American Eagle" on the daily call sheets, and Spielberg thinks he sounds so authoritative he keeps coming up with new lines of dialogue for him to say.

The module behind Truffaut is rigged with special 'sugar' glass. When the Mothership plays an especially loud note the glass will shatter all over the hangar. Rather than cut the shot Spielberg pays for the glass himself. It's several thousand dollars a sheet, and we do three takes before Spielberg's satisfied.

Spielberg cast Phil Dodds in his role of the ARP player when Dodds came to Mobile to install the ARP. If he looks anxious here, it's because he told his boss he'd only be filming for two weeks, and we're falling behind schedule. He's due back in Boston and the Mothership hasn't even landed yet.

We've just put on our sunglasses and are running forward to get a better look at the Mothership. Banks of incredibly bright lights are being aimed at us, and Spielberg is calling out directions: "It's about fifteen feet up, and you've never seen anything this big in your life."

Here we're all lined up pretending to watch the Mothership land. Actually, we're being zapped by incredibly bright lights so Steven can film the 'landing lights' shining on our faces. The camera is up on a scaffolding with the lights so Steven can film us from the Mothership's point of view.

The Mothership has finally landed, and we're filming longshots of our reactions to it. A giant crane is holding it up, and it's taken several days to just move the ship into the hangar. The whole thing weighs almost twenty tons. Joe Alves has made it out of steel, since special effects will add on the rest of the ship later, and the edges mustn't waver or bend during filming.

A closeup of the Big Set model built by Joe Alves, the production designer. Spielberg would move the little men around like toy soldiers to figure out camera positions and line up shots. Note the technicians's modules lining the set. No one realized the Mobile weather would be hot enough to melt their plastic walls.

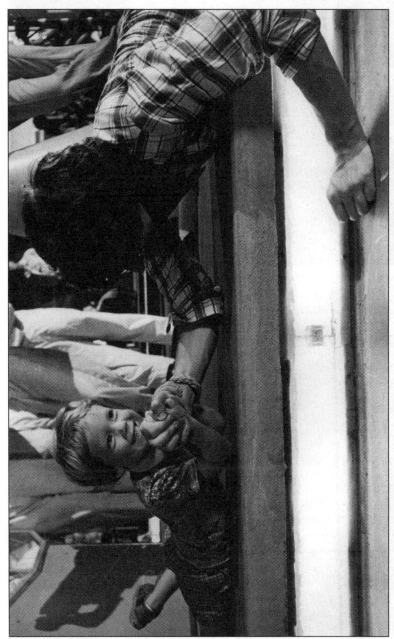

Steven and Cary are horsing around on the Big Set. Steven found this talented kid in Atlanta, Georgia after a nationwide search. The crew called him "One-take" Guffey, because he could do everything Steven wanted on the first take.

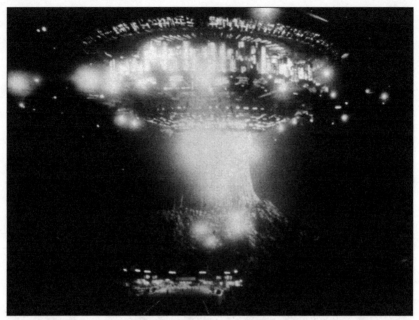

Well here it is, the fantastic Mothership landing. We're ants in the distance; special effects has reduced us optically. The Mothership has been built to look like a city. When they constructed the buildings on it, they used to refer to it by street names, like "Broadway". If we had only known what this would look like!

This says it all. A shot like this makes it well worth the hot, Mobile summer and endless looking up at... nothing... in a sweltering airplane hangar. Everything above the horizon line is special effects, but the whole landing strip area was really there, reduced optically until we looked miniaturized.

Every one of the returnees had to have a transparency taken and put on this light board. A photographer worked for weeks making portraits of each returnee, in case Steven decided to shoot a closeup of one of them.

The returnees arrive! These are the people who have mysteriously disappeared through the ages. Amelia Earhart returns, along with Judge Crater, and a flight of World War II fighter pilots missing in action. If you look carefully, in the left foreground is makeup man/actor, Bob Westmoreland, who is dressed as an English sea captain.

Here are the little six year-old girls dressed in their ET costumes. Originally, their costumes were to have radio controlled eyes, but the rubber heads proved too heavy for the little kids to wear. We had to keep re-shooting this scene because the kids kept disco dancing.

# POST-PRODUCTION

Principal photography was over in September, 1976, but we waited for a short scene which was to be filmed in India. We waited through September and then October, and finally January, 1977 arrived and we still hadn't seen India. We began to think of the trip as rumor, until we arrived in Bombay at the end of February, 1977 and spent five days trying not to drink the water or get bitten by anything poisonous. We finished, said goodbye, and thought we'd meet again at the première of the movie. In May, however, we were called to film additional scenes. Columbia executives had screened the movie in a rough cut and loved it. They told Spielberg to film whatever scenes he wanted and we soon found ourselves getting blasted by a sand-storm in the Mojave desert, filming a new beginning to the movie. We then spent several days on the sound stage in Hollywood filming more added scenes. When we finally said goodbye at the Burbank Studios, I don't think any of us really believed the movie was finally over.

Here's the Indian leader teaching three thousand extras the wrong five notes. He never could get the music right, and throughout the afternoon assistant directors kept rushing up to him between takes and singing the correct notes in his ear. It never worked. Spielberg had to dub in the notes months later on a Hollywood soundstage.

Spielberg wanted a shot of these extras pointing up at the sky, but he had to do a lot of takes before he got what he wanted. Each time the camera rolled one of the extras forgot to put his hand up at the right moment, or somebody pointed in the wrong direction.

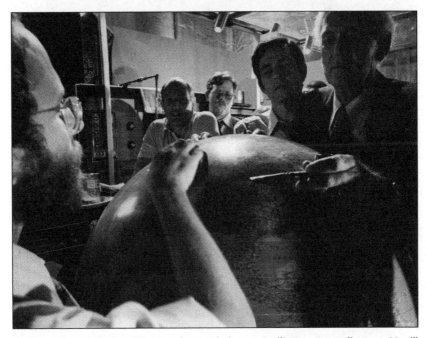

Here I am at the Burbank Studios a year later, pointing out Devil's Tower's coordinates to Merrill Connally. This year, Steven has changed my profession from interpreter to cartographer. Perhaps it's because I don't parle francais well enough?

We're filming Truffaut's entrance. Spielberg had to lay dolly tracks for the camera, since the ground didn't provide a flat enough surface. Later on we film us walking backwards between the tracks and looking up at the sky while Fuller's Earth engulfs me. We had to keep filming that sequence over and over because walking backwards through the dolly tracks made me look like a geisha girl.

It is a year later in the Mojave desert, and this new scene introducing me to François Truffaut, replaces the airport scene. Even though this is the opening scene of the movie, it was one of the last scenes shot.

Spielberg still doesn't look tired. We're breaking for lunch, and he's out with the planes lining up shots. The rest of us are trying to get the dirt out of our hair.

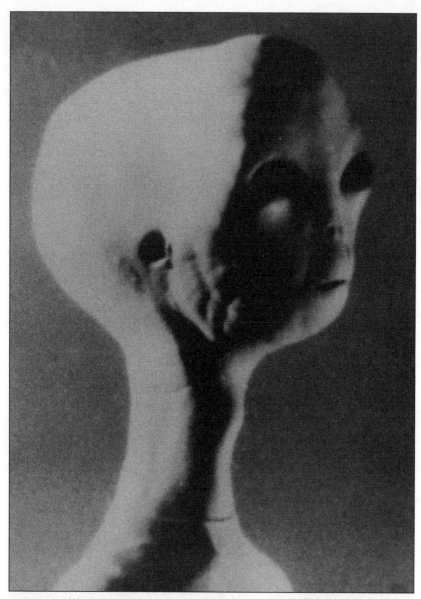

Carlo Rambaldi built this extraterrestrial almost a year after filming in Mobile was completed. It's connected to an elaborate system of levers, and seven or eight technicians are pulling and turning handles which operate the creature. This ET can even wink and bob its Adam's apple.

Dreyfuss is filming his "mashed potato" section of the movie. The shape of Devil's Tower has invaded his consciousness and everything reminds him of the mountain.

Melinda and Dreyfuss help Cary with his sandcastle between takes. For the rest of us the movie was sometimes hot and tedious. But for Cary it was a fun day at the playground.

Here's Steven exhibiting his natural "fatherly" instincts. Steven loved playing with Cary and Cary was especially fond of Steven.

Vilmos and Steven line up another shot of Devil's Tower, while the weather holds. Later they take pictures of sleeping animals, who are currently waiting off-screen for their big moment.

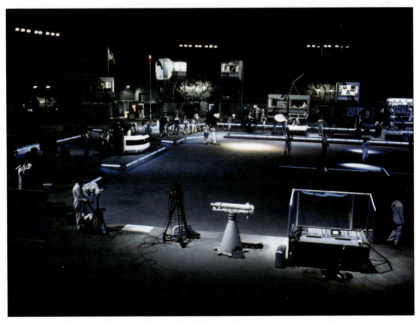

On the Big Set, waiting for the Mothership. The scene was shot from every conceivable angle, and the temperature got well above one hundred degrees.

Little Cary waits happily for the aliens to take him away. Even from behind you can sense how relaxed and trusting he was — I don't think the movie could have been made without this amazing little boy.

We are all getting blasted by light from the Mothership which has finally landed. I'm glad we're wearing sunglasses. The lights were so bright some of the footage got fogged and we had to reshoot.

I look happy, but I'm really afraid of getting bitten by a malaria-carrying mosquito, out in the boonies of Bombay. This is one day I avoid the food.

The milling throng of local Indian extras, waiting around for lunch. India produces more movies than any country in the world — and our tireless crew seemed thrilled to appear in one.

Steven directs thousands of extras. There's no shade, no wind, and a lot of dust, but Steven never appears uncomfortable, and never loses his cool.

Soon after this picture was taken, Truffaut collapsed from the heat and had to be revived. Fortunately he quickly recovered, and there was no lasting damage, except a fear of the Indian countryside.

We clown around in the shade of the trees that were our dressing rooms. I fought to have an "equal facilities" clause in my contract, so Truffaut and I got similar sized trees.

These next three photos I took with my Brownie. We're at the hotel, and Truffaut is pretending to look dignified. He sits next to Steven and his translator, Françoise Forget. Later we all go shopping behind the hotel and buy rubies and antiques. You'd think we were having fun.

Truffaut makes his traditional "you may be taking a picture of me, but I'm really taking a picture of you" gesture, as we wait for a shot. He loved watching Steven work, and wrote letters to his daughters about his experience on the set. They were huge Spielberg fans.

Back at the hotel. Notice how Steven is smartly avoiding the sun, of which we have all had too much. He's reading a potential movie property he was considering.

## JULY 28

I go to Doug Trumbull's office, upstairs in the hangar. It's small and unglamorous because Doug does most of his work back in Los Angeles at his company, Future General. He explains to me he's been making electronic cuboids back at Future General using a computerized animation technique called 'synthevision'. He will superimpose the animated cuboids over shots of our reactions. Since the cuboids won't be traveling in straight rows across the camera but will circle about and travel at all sorts of angles, he will use the computer to print-out two dimensional cuboids to match the three dimensional cuboids we've been filming in perspective and velocity.

He will make little pin holes in the backs of the film on every cuboid and shine a bright light through them, so a tiny little flare will be produced to correspond to the flare of the cuboids we are filming today. My head is reeling. Doug shows me photos of miles of miniature countryside he's using as background for the scenes on Crescendo Summit where Melinda finds Cary Guffey and meets Richard for the first time.

The actual mountain is still being built in the hangar near the Big Set. This miniature will be projected on to a screen as background for the scene. It looks terrific with its little houses and mailboxes and winding roads. Doug says he's still working on the stars. He says Steven is very particular about the stars.

## JULY 29

Heard a rumor last week that Spielberg wasn't happy with the airport limousine scene. It's true. Spielberg says that it's not our fault — he likes the acting in the scene. The problem is that he never filmed closeups or additional angles, and the scene has a very static look to it. Today we will film closeups in a small building near the hangar.

Truffaut and I have been in Mobile for almost six weeks. After this scene we get to go away for a few days, so we can't wait to finish it. We're called to the set a little early and watch Melinda filming an added scene.

She is in a New Mexican-style hotel room watching Devil's Tower appear on the news. The room is filled with tacky, pseudo-Western furniture and the camera crew is placing bets on who gets to keep the Gene Autry lamp. Spielberg has decided he wants it to be raining outside the motel set, so the special effects crew is rigging hoses to keep up a steady stream of water outside the window. Spielberg is working with Melinda. This is the mountain she has been fixating on throughout the movie, and here it is in the flesh, so to speak. Melinda is to react, run to the wall and touch some of the pictures of the Tower she has been drawing. It is an extremely difficult scene to do. Especially at eight o'clock in the morning. She watches the videotape and bursts into tears over and over again as Spielberg works to get just the right camera moves. Before each take he goes over to Melinda and whispers something. She is able to repeat the emotionally draining scene about fifteen times, until Spielberg is finally satisfied with the take. Melinda says Spielberg is incredibly intuitive about how to speak to her before a difficult scene.

It's time for Truffaut and Lance and me to repeat our car sequence* and we get into the limousine one more time as the set crew mops up the water from the rain in Melinda's scene. This time we are in front of a piece of black velour instead of at the airport. We repeat the scene a few times, and then do our closeups quickly. Truffaut is wonderful; he appears to be inventing his lines as he speaks, and Spielberg suggests I adopt Truffaut's halting style when I do my closeup. I do, and it goes very well. We finish, and say goodbye for a week. The set crew is transporting the Mothership into the Big Set from an adjoining hangar, and it will take a few days to adjust the twenty-ton creation and to re-light.

I'm going home to New York, and Truffaut is off to Beverly Hills. He loves California. He's looking forward to spending a lot of time in Larry Edmund's theater bookstore, and driving around in his convertible. (Truffaut loves convertibles and tried to rent one in Mobile, but the closest thing he could find was a Hornet with a sunroof.) We make plans to go to the airport when Spielberg comes over with the bad news — Truffaut must stay for a few more hours and miss his plane to L.A. A retake of his reaction to Richard and Melinda escaping to Devil's Tower must be reshot again. Someone made a mistake and the venetian blinds were up instead of down; the closeup doesn't match the shot we did in Wyoming. I sympathize with Truffaut and leave for home. He goes sadly off to Wardrobe.

## AUGUST 2

Richard and his girlfriend Lucinda Valles went to a local bar last night in the nice part of town to have drinks with Richard's friend Carl Borack. A very drunk person came up to Richard and did the "Aren't you the one with the shark?" routine. Richard politely said yes, and went back to his drink, but the guy wouldn't leave him alone. He kept saying how wonderful it was to see Richard and how great he thinks Richard is. As he was talking, he kept punching Richard on the arm and shaking him by the shoulders.

Finally, the bartender had to come over to make the man stop bothering Richard. Richard says he is beginning to develop a fear of public places.

---

Today weird flying objects are pursuing everyone around the Big Set. We don't actually see any of these things of course, but Steven keeps describing what they will look like; which ones are frightening, and which ones are nice. The light crew has placed four men in a tram that is strung along the ceiling. Four massive lights are hung from it. As the objects supposedly fly overhead, the tram zooms by and shines the lights at us. Later, when the effects are put in, it will seem as if the lights are coming from the UFOs.

Melinda's son, Richie, is visiting the Big Set today. Truffaut says he'd like Richie to direct him in the movie for a while. He tells Richie to watch him intently, and anything Richie tells him to do, he'll do. Richie takes this very seriously and studies Truffaut for a few takes. He then instructs him on where to hold his hands, when to start moving, and what exactly his glance should be like. Truffaut follows his directions exactly. They are quite good.

The extras are given measuring devices and are told to run to certain parts of the set and wave them around excitedly. A lot of them think this is very funny, and Steven has to stop shooting every time one of them breaks up. Actually, it is pretty funny to see a bunch of grown-up men dashing around a deserted airplane hangar shaking a lot of fancy eggbeaters at thin air. Special Effects has put air ducts around the set, and as extras dressed as scientists run over them, the air shoots up and sends their papers flying. It will look as though the UFO flying overhead had degravitized them. Some of us are rigged with air jets in our costumes, so that when the UFOs fly overhead our hair will appear to stand on end. My hair can't stand on end in Mobile because there is too much humidity.

Some of the extras run across the air jets half-heartedly. One of the ADs gets carried away and gives them a peptalk that sounds more like a tonguelashing. It is hot and crowded and smoky, and tempers are short. The extras grumble and start gathering in small clusters to talk about mutiny.

They have recently caught on to the pecking order: since it is very hot in the hangar, and takes a long time to set up, there is something of a ritual as to whom comes on the set first. The film crew comes first and lines up the shot. The extras are then brought in and placed in their approximate positions. Then the scene is lit, and the film crew checks everything out. Then there is re-lighting. This can take a long time, and it is *very* hot in the hangar. Finally the actors are called. Those who have been hired for only a couple of weeks arrive first. Then Lance and I are called, then Truffaut. Truffaut usually has to wait five or ten minutes, but the extras often have to wait over an hour until the shot actually begins. And Richard is not called until after Truffaut is on the set. Richard is called when everyone is in position, and we are really ready to begin filming.

Anyway, the extras now realize they are doing a lot of unnecessary waiting. And they resent being yelled at. Later that afternoon they call a meeting with the production staff to voice their grievances. I have a vision of the extras taking over the Mothership.

## AUGUST 3

Richard has been doing a lot of run-bys in his truck. Run-bys are shots where you film something that's passing from one side of the frame to the other. They're bits of action which come between dialogue. They usually go by very quickly in the film but Richard says that the scenes that look dramatic and hard are the easiest and nicest to do. It's the run-bys in the trucks that are impossible.

He's already filmed the scene in which Neary pulls up to a railroad crossing, takes out his map to examine it and has an encounter with a UFO. The interior of the cab will be filmed weeks later. Richard says he was sitting on a deserted Mobile road for hours in the cab of the truck with all the movie lights directed at him, attracting every insect from Pennsylvania on south. Richard says he hardly remembers the scene. For him, the sequence was about sitting in the middle of six trillion bugs.

They also filmed the sequence where he motions the car lights behind him to pass and they start rising over him. They raised the lights on a forklift truck. Richard says when he first read the script, that was one of his favorite scenes. He could *hear* the audience reacting. The first time they did it the lights came closer and closer, and then a little closer, and then they smashed right into the truck. An encounter of the too close kind?

## AUGUST 4

Returnees are returning again today. The ETs have a couple of days off and Susan says she's glad because they had been getting very hot and very tired.

About sixty extras are getting outfitted for their slow march out of the Mothership. The makeup man will be a returnee today. Since the moment he found out that he would be in the scene he has been experimenting with makeup and hair so that nobody will recognize him from his scene with Richard at the power plant. I don't think anybody will. He has dyed his hair

MOBILE, ALABAMA

black, and is wearing an enormous moustache. He has developed an authentic British accent for his part of a Sea Captain, even though he will have no lines. He runs around checking himself in mirrors and asking everyone he sees if they like his makeup. Twin eight year-old girls in Milk Maid costumes come in to have their hair braided, and Amelia Earhart's second double is having her long hair pinned up under her bright hat.

I say hello to two friends of Steven's, Matthew Robbins and Hal Barwood, who wrote *The Sugarland Express*. They have come to Mobile to be returnees. They thought they would be here for two days, and today is their fourth day. Matt speaks terrific French, and has a nice conversation with Truffaut. I fear he may speak French better than I do. Bruce Davison is here, too. His house is next to Steven's in L.A., and the two have become friendly across pools.

ADs with walkie-talkies circulate around the outskirts of the hangar, calling everyone to the set. Fortunately, the returnees won't make their entrance until after the Mothership has already landed and opened, so temperatures inside the ship won't be quite as terrible. They scramble up to a waiting platform inside the ship and wait for Steven to call action. Foggers start up their machines. Truffaut and I take our places next to the ARP, and the technician extras fan out behind us.

The fog rolls in and the returnees start exiting. They must walk very carefully, because even with the rubber on the bottom of their shoes the ramp is very slippery. Steven does not want anyone to come out feet first. Steven has given everyone instructions to look a little dazed, so they all look numbly around. Matt and Hal are among the first to exit. They are interviewed by a waiting officer, and give their names and ranks and are shunted off to get debriefed. They are really good even though they've never acted before. There is a lot of coverage from a lot of angles. In between takes, people with long-handled mops and Windex remove scuffmarks from the mylar surface.

Finally the returnees are sent back to Wardrobe. The makeup man has completed his entrance, but goes around for the rest of the day dressed in his Sea Captain outfit, talking with a British accent.

The fog starts again. The camera is re-positioned in front of the Mothership, the lights gleam brightly and Elmer comes tumbling down the silver ramp, mostly on his backside. He tries to get his footing but it's impossible, so he just leans back and enjoys the ride. He gets to the bottom, barks, and runs over to Steven to lick his face. Close Encounters of the FURRED Kind?

117

**AUGUST 5**

Elvis appeared in town last night. You couldn't get within three blocks of the auditorium. We're shooting there today, and I make my way over mounds of paper cups to the honeywagons stationed behind the hall.

The crew is removing Elvis' stage and erecting a dignified platform for Truffaut and the rest of our delegation. We're doing the scene in which Truffaut explains to the technicians the Zoltan Kodaly hand-signals we will use to communicate with the ETs at the end of the film. As soon as we're out of makeup we're sent over to Steven to be taught the signals. Steven is very patient as he demonstrates them to us: "No, François, thumbs up on the last signal, and a little slower." Steven explains they are visual representations of the five notes we will have heard in India.

Johnny Williams came by last week and brought Spielberg several different five note combinations from which to choose the five notes we will use to communicate with the Mothership. Spielberg sings us the one he's chosen. There's something inevitable about the sequence. As we practice our hand signals we sing along with appropriate notes.

Truffaut confides that he is very worried today. He has more English dialogue in this scene than in any other, and he has been up all night practicing. We go over his lines a few times and he asks me to correct his pronunciation which I hesitate to do because I find his fractured English adorable.

We go into the auditorium and watch Steven giving instructions to the extras who are lined up in rows in front of the stage. He says it's important that they don't all react in a clump. He wants some to applaud, some to cheer, and some to stand up when Truffaut makes his announcement.

Truffaut and I climb onto the stage. I start talking with some of the extras. They are playing FBI men and look very official. I ask one of the men what he does and he explains he *is* an FBI man. He has just chased a gangster from Texas to the Canadian border. He says he's pretty tired today but would not miss being in a movie for anything. He says the guy he was chasing was some kind of a Rolls Royce smuggler, but says it would be improper to tell me all the details.

Truffaut runs over to me to remind him how to pronounce the word "something" and we take our places. In the first shot Truffaut goes over to the podium, introduces himself, and asks if the audience speaks French. This goes very smoothly, and after two or three takes Steven is satisfied and we move in for Truffaut's closeup. Truffaut asks if he could perhaps say his long speech in French and I could translate, but Spielberg says no. He wants Truffaut to speak English here. Truffaut goes back and forth behind the podium rehearsing his speech to himself, wildly exaggerating his English pronunciation. He sounds more French than ever. Spielberg yells "Action!" and the take begins. Truffaut approaches the podium shyly. He opens his notebook, clears his throat and looks up at the audience. He begins flawlessly. He says his first two sentences, and it's clear that he's home free. And then he gets to the word "today" and starts stumbling over it. First he emphasizes the wrong syllable. Then he says the word again and tries to correct himself and breaks himself up. He just cannot get past that word. Spielberg keeps filming. He loves it when people make mistakes. If Truffaut doesn't stop, Steven is liable to use this take. Truffaut comes to a dead halt, looks up smiling, and says in halting English, "Ziss iss terrible." Everybody laughs and we begin again.

---

Teri told me the following story at dinner tonight: Teri is with Melinda with her eight year-old son, Richie, at the hotel pool. Melinda sends Richie up to the room to get a portable radio. He's gone for a while, and all of a sudden he sticks his head out the window and screams hysterically. Melinda runs up the six flights to the room.

It seems two men have called on the telephone and told Richie they were going to arrest his mother for keeping guns and ammunition in the room, which, of course, she hadn't been doing. While she is in jail they say they will put Richie in a special place where they keep children of bad parents — a detention home. Richie kept thinking they had the wrong number, but they knew his name and they told him to stay on the phone while they came up to get him, because they were in the hotel. That's when Richie ran to the window screaming for his mother.

Melinda and Richie went downstairs to the switchboard and asked if their room had gotten any calls in the last few hours. They tell her that no calls had come in from outside; if anybody's called, it's been from inside the hotel.

So Julia hires some more guards to take care of Richie and Melinda. One of the guards keeps flashing his gun around, making everyone nervous, but the other is very friendly and nice. And when we all go out to dinner together, we take the nice guard with us and leave the one with the gun back at the hotel to guard the room. The guards spend a lot of time sitting in the room next to Melinda's, waiting for the kidnappers, but they're never heard from again. It occurs to me that the head of the local Guarding Business in Mobile may be making all the threats.

## AUGUST 6

Dreyfuss comes back from work today reeling. He's been filming the sequence in the cab of his truck in which the UFO passes overhead, and everything in the cab starts flying all over the place. They attached the cab and the camera to a turning platform, strapped Richard in, and rotated everything like a chicken on a spit. Since the camera revolved along with the cab, he will look like he's right side up. He says after four times of turning upside down he began to get very nauseous. He can't imagine how Fred Astaire survived the same camera trick when he danced around the ceiling in *Royal Wedding*.

## AUGUST 7

We are filming what feels like the ninetieth take of a shot in which Truffaut and Lance and I walk a few feet to the left and notice something. I think it's supposed to be a flashing red ball, but it may be a cuboid egg. We've been pretending to see so many flying objects that it's hard to keep them straight.

One of the overhead lights shorts out, and the head gaffer says we're going to have to break for fifteen minutes. We go to the hangar entrance to wait. It is broiling hot. I grab an ice cream bar on the way, and Truffaut shoots me a disapproving look. He says I'll get fat if I keep eating like this, and he's probably right, but I don't care. Dreyfuss has ordered a case of ice cream to thank everyone for working so hard throughout this heat and to provide a little boost in company morale. A uniformed ice cream man stands by, cheerfully refilling any item that is running low. This is the first time in my life I have an unlimited supply of popsicles.

I ask Truffaut if he believes in UFOs. Truffaut says maybe, maybe not; he's not really interested in them. He feels he has to be very selective about his interests. He says he has about thirty more years to make movies, and he wants to concentrate on the things that are important to him. He explains that there are only three things in life he is really interested in: movies, relationships between men and women, and children.

## AUGUST 8

Richard says that sometimes its hard to believe people are actually paying him to go "——" (He does the famous *CE3K* stare from left to right.) He says that to him, *Close Encounters* is standing on mountains, sitting in cars, crouching in hangars in 120 degree heat, looking at absolutely... NOTHING!

## AUGUST 9

We're filming the 'jam session' with the Mothership, where the UFO communicates with us in a musical conversation. Johnny Williams oversees as we take our positions around the ARP. During the sequence Phil Dodds will play the ARP and the giant lightboard behind us will light up. Actually he'll be synching the ARP to pre-recorded music. Nevertheless, he's had to learn the music since his fingers are supposed to look like they're hitting the correct notes. Phil hasn't had the music very long, and he's a little nervous. He also wants to go home.

I asked Joe Alves about the lightboard. He wanted to use a television device to communicate with the Mothership, but Spielberg wanted the scaffolding look of a scoreboard — he didn't want a "spacey" look. Joe was looking for a way to link the music with the colors on the scoreboard. He was sitting watching Leonard Bernstein doing a lecture on Schoenberg and got the idea to work colors on a 12-tone scale. He realized that there are twelve perfect steps in a secondary color progression going from yellow, through the color wheel, and eventually back to yellow again. He took pure, middle range yellow and related it to middle C; an octave higher would be a lighter tone of yellow. He ended up with 72 notes and 72 corresponding colors. Then he built a piano with 72 notes. If you hit "Q" it would strike a little circuit which would then turn on the yellow light for middle C. There was a person playing the 'piano' in one of the modules, and he played the same music as the ARP player, and made the colors light on the board.

Steven stations us around the ARP. We're wearing headsets, but they don't plug into anything, and as we walk around we get tangled in our wires. Finally I plug my headset into my shoe. People make last minute checks on the elaborate circuitry that attaches the piano to the lightboard. The ADs position the sea of extras behind us. The piano player hides in the module, and Phil Dodds takes his position behind the ARP. There is a battery of arc lights aimed at us; when the Mothership answers our notes she will respond with colors as well, and these colors must be seen reflecting off our faces. We're ready for a take; the cameras begin to roll.

Phil plays the five notes and the Mothership lets out with a long low tuba note that sounds like gas. Everyone laughs. Phil plays some more notes and the Mothership starts answering, almost playfully. The music gets faster and faster. Dodds is back there really sweating, but he's keeping up. The lights are synchronizing perfectly, and it's a pleasure to hear the score filling the hangar. When the take is over, everyone applauds.

**AUGUST 10**

Merrill Connally's nephew is coming to watch us work today. He is even taller than Merrill, if this is possible. The two of them almost have to fold in two to get into the car. We talk about the movie, and how much Merrill misses his cattle ranch. I sit there trying to remember if it's the beginning or the end of the week.

We're doing more reactions to ETs today. There is a rumor that there was so much fog and so much glare from the lights in the Mothership, that the ETs have been totally invisible for the last two days, and we may have to re-do their entrance.

---

We're almost finished on the Big Set. Maybe. More extras are quitting. Some of them have previous job commitments. Others are hot and tired, and don't really care whether Steven has to juggle shots to avoid the lack of crowd in the background. We're filming people in steaming modules, and some medium closeups of crowd reactions. We've finished filming the Mothership, but it's still sitting in the middle of the hangar, because it would take time to remove it, and everybody wants to be out of here as quickly as possible.

Teri stops by the set to say hello. She has been sitting around Mobile waiting to do more work in the Neary house. In the meantime she's been going to museums, driving around to local shopping centers. She has stopped at every historical point of interest in Mobile. Ladies in hoop skirts and make-believe curls have been showing her through miniature Taras. Teri imitates these ladies in a pinched, high voice and thick Southern accent: "Thiz wuz Miz Sarah Belle's tea set, and thiz wuz huh silvah." She is going crazy here.

Spielberg films a shot in which the glass front of one of the modules shatters from the effect of an incredibly loud note from the Mothership. The studio wanted Steven to drop the shot and refused to give him the money for the special sugar glass required for the effect. Steven feels it is a really important moment in the film and has paid for the glass himself. We all gather in the Big Set to watch the effect, and hide behind some benches as a crew member waits in the module for a signal to hit the glass. It breaks and showers splinters all around the set. It's three takes and three panes of glass before Spielberg is happy with the shot. It has cost him almost $10,000.

## AUGUST 11

Spielberg says we'll finish on the Big Set this week. I hope he's right. The extras are getting restless, and soon there won't be many left.

On the drive to work this morning, poor Phil Dodds was upset. They told him he had to be back at his job at ARP this week, but Spielberg hasn't finished shooting him yet. He keeps trying to find someone who will tell him when he can go home, but no one really knows. Every day he gets a threatening call from his boss. Yesterday he got a load of work from his office with a note saying things were piling up. He takes out his notebook between shots and tries to work on circuitry problems in machines in Boston. He's losing weight. Everybody keeps telling him how wonderful he is in the dailies. This doesn't help. He wants to go home. He's already finished the entire *Foundation Trilogy*, and lends it to me.

I'm getting anxious to finish, too, but I realize it's hopeless to worry about it. They will finish when they finish. Truffaut has just returned from a few days in L.A. and sent back a load of books from Larry Edmunds. He's got one for everybody on the film and they're all inscribed. He gives me a copy of his collected screenplays and I race to my trailer to read the inscription. The inscription in the first book he gave me was warmer. He may not like me anymore. I tell myself how insane I'm being. It doesn't help. I don't think Truffaut likes me. Maybe we have just been cooped up too long in this hangar. I tell myself how paranoid I'm being, when Lance runs over to me. Truffaut has given him a copy of *The 400 Blows* with a wonderful inscription. I am tremendously jealous. Truffaut is allowed to like whomever he wants, I think; I am acting like a crazy person. I sulk in my trailer for the next few hours.

Finally I'm called to the set around five. The extraterrestrials are working for their last day and we're doing closeups of them as they surround Truffaut and me and Richard and Dr. Hynek. I watch as two or three little ETs hover over Dreyfuss. They touch his hair and reach out their hands to his. They are very sweet looking. Richard watches them, amazed, as Spielberg calls out, "Fast hands, now... don't touch him so hard, Kim... everybody run away." The same thing is repeated with Truffaut and me. Then with Dr. Hynek.* I love watching this scientist surrounded by Outerspacelings. He reacts to them almost reverentially as they remove his silver glasses and gently place them back on his head. Then Spielberg does some insert closeups. The kids are wearing hands without joints, but for the insert Spielberg will use a mechanical hand that bends at the knuckles and is able to grasp things. I'm feeling a little less crazy now. Truffaut and I discuss how tired we are after all this time, and how we are looking forward to going home. Julia's assistant

Kendall Cooper comes over to me and says that Julia would like to see me in her office. I can't imagine what she wants to talk to me about. Perhaps she has noticed that my hair was completely straight in Wyoming, and frizzy in Mobile and will never match. We march into her office.

Julia explains she would like to film the India sequence in the beginning of October instead of the middle of September. There's a slight problem. Truffaut's film *Small Change* is opening the New York Film Festival on October 6th and he is planning on being there. Julia would like me to talk to Truffaut and see if he'd be willing to change his mind. She asks me to interpret for her and says maybe if the three of us sit down and talk about it we can work things out. I'm flattered that she thinks I can influence Truffaut, but I know how much he wants to be at the Festival, and I tell her I doubt if I can help. Five minutes later Truffaut and I are sitting in Julia's office and I'm translating. Julia explains how really great it would be for the film if Truffaut could go to India in October, and François is explaining how terrible it would be for him. Everybody is smiling a lot, but nobody's changing their mind. I am trying to be extremely precise in my translation efforts. I love being the interpreter and hope that negotiations continue for a while. I'm really getting into this.

Everyone agrees to think things over. I wonder how much interpreters make an hour?

---

Mike Kahn, the editor, and Spielberg have a terrific working relationship. He says that they were sitting around one night having dinner together, and Spielberg told him how he grew up in Phoenix; Kahn said he grew up in Brooklyn. Spielberg told Kahn how he was a Boy Scout; that's how he got involved with film — he was working on a merit badge. Kahn told Spielberg that he was a Boy Scout, too. Then Spielberg said that he was an Eagle Scout. Kahn said he was an Eagle Scout as well. Then Spielberg said that he was in the 'Order of the Arrow', a secret honor society; Kahn said so was he. So Spielberg said "Michael, I am something that you're not. I'm a Sagittarian." And Kahn said, "Well, Steven, so am I."

## AUGUST 12

Steven has been shooting on Crescendo Summit. He is shooting on the set, rather than on location, so he can control conditions for the special effects which will be added later. They've already filmed the scene where Neary is supposed to speed through the Summit in his truck and almost run over

Barry. Joe Alves explains that cars can usually only be driven slowly on a set because there's not enough room to pick up speed. They generally film the car driving quickly through an exterior and then cut to the car puffing slowly onto the set. But there are two large doors at either end of the Crescendo Summit hangar, so Joe has begun his road at one door and ended it at the other. Neary's truck will enter the hangar at top speed, drive through the set at over fifty miles per hour, and exit through the door at the other end. Later, a sequence where a helicopter lands on the summit will be filmed outside because even Steven can't fly a helicopter in a hangar.

The special effects people get the front-screen projection system ready. The Crescendo Summit sequence will have one of the largest front-screen projections ever used in a film. The screen on which the images will be projected is so large that it got bent during shipment, and it's taking a crew of men five days to get the thing straight again.

A smaller screen is being set up behind the Big Set. When Richard and Melinda first reach the top of Devil's Tower and look down at the landing strip below, they will be looking at front-screen projections. I ask someone to show me how the projector works. It's amazing. In rearscreen projection, you stand in front of a screen that has pictures projected onto it from behind. But the screen causes a slight blue outline in flare out around whatever is in front of it, which makes it impossible to disguise the fact that it's a process shot. In front-screen projection, the image is thrown onto the screen from a projector attached to the camera, and the process is virtually undetectable.

I have never understood why, in front projection, if people walk in front of projections of the Alps you don't see mountains on their noses. Nick McLean, the camera operator, explained that actually you do, only the image is very, very faint and you don't notice it. The secret of all this magic is two-fold: 1) the screen that is used for this process is very special; it's also very expensive — it is made to reflect and amplify any light striking it with amazing fidelity and force; and 2) it will only reflect light forward. It does not refract light.

In other words, if you stand to the side of a scene being shot in front-screen projection, you will see actors in front of a big black screen. If you put your eye very close to the camera lens, you can make out a dim background. The projection is focused so that the brightest, clearest image is aimed directly at the lens, and only when the film is projected will you be able to see the background in full effect.

I'm ready for my PhD.

**AUGUST 13**

**Miscellany:**

... We're supposed to finish on the Big Set today. I don't think we will. The tarpaulin blew off again yesterday, and the Mothership is now exposed to the threatening Mobile sky. Steven has decided to shoot inserts of people turning dials in the modules until the crew can get the tarp back together again. It may take days.

---

... Dreyfuss tells me he first heard about *Close Encounters of the Third Kind* during *Jaws*. He says that Spielberg sat around the kitchen table on Martha's Vineyard and told this incredible story, and they were all spellbound. He says Spielberg is a *great* storyteller. Months later, back in Los Angeles, Spielberg sent Dreyfuss the script. He read it and thought it was the best idea for a movie he'd ever read in his life and he would schnorr, hondel, convince, blackmail or do whatever he had to do to get the part. After weeks of 120 degree heat and looking up at imaginary UFOs, I wonder if Dreyfuss really remembers what it felt like to want to be here.

---

... We have a new publicity person. The original publicity person was told to keep publicity to a minimum, but he has taken his job too seriously. We are about to complete production and nothing at all has been written about the movie. So today there is an influx of media. No one is actually allowed on the Big Set, and none of us are to tell anyone anything about the movie, so I'm not sure what the journalists will be writing about.

---

... Melinda and I talk about how difficult it is to react to off-screen flying objects that aren't really there. Melinda says that Steven was very helpful when they filmed her reaction to the arrival of the Mothership. She says she'd been up on her Devil's Tower rock for two days, with no idea of what was going on, but Spielberg coached her through the shot. She says she felt like she was Lillian Gish and Spielberg was D.W. Griffith. Spielberg told her to think of the most extravagant, frightening, closest thing to her heart. He told her to turn away from the camera, and he started talking about how she would turn back and look at the piece of paper he was holding and see the biggest, the most wondrous thing she has ever seen. She says he just kept saying things like that, and as she turned around she saw her dead grandmother at the age of thirty; a beautiful woman looming over the set, and saw herself as a little girl. She gasped and said, "Oh, my God!" — just the reaction Steven wanted.

---

... Joe Hyams comes by to do in-depth interviews with the actors. We started speaking this morning at makeup, continued at lunch, and I'm only just getting to the part where I'm in my first New York play. This afternoon, we all go up to Steven's office for our filmed interviews. They will be held by Columbia until after the movie is released. We sit in Steven's office under very bright lights and the man behind the camera asks questions like, "Did you ever see a UFO?" "Would you *like* to see a UFO?" and, "Did anything unusual happen during the course of the filming involving UFOs?" He makes the movie sound like *It Came From Outer Space*.

---

... Steven films Melinda's and Cary's reactions to the Mothership leaving. They rehearse for a few minutes. Steven yells, "Action", and Barry runs into his mother's arms. Spielberg has told Cary to say things. "Did you see me up there?" and "I went with my friends," and amazingly, Cary remembers everything. Steven wants Cary to be sad his new extraterrestrial friends are going away. He tells Cary to turn around and say "My friends are leaving," as the Mothership takes off. Cary turns to say this and bursts out crying. Melinda didn't know he was going to cry, and when she sees him crying, she starts to cry, too. It's a lovely moment. I can't believe how lucky Spielberg was to get this wonderful kid.

---

... I speak to Janet Maslin from *Newsweek*, but since I'm not supposed to reveal anything about the movie, I confine myself to what a wonderful time I'm having, how nice everybody is, and how well everything's going. It's a lot like letters from camp. Steven is speaking this afternoon to a reporter from the

*Washington Post.* It will be the first interview he's given to anyone since filming began. I pass by the reporter, and overhear
Steven telling him the entire plot of the movie in great detail.

---

... The astronauts are in their shiny red flight suits, waiting to
film their march onto the Mothership. They've been filming the
"last rites" sequence with a real Catholic priest who arrived late
because he was performing a wedding. The astronauts have been
cooped up in the module all morning, and some of them faint
from the heat and lack of air. One of the astronauts is a woman
who appeared on the set wearing the biggest beehive hairdo I've
ever seen. Edie the hairdresser follows her around all day trying
to make her hair look smaller. Nothing works. When she finally
boards the Mothership, she looks like Zsa Zsa Gabor on her way
to a taping of *The Tonight Show.*

## AUGUST 16

We have had our "last day" on the Big Set for the last three days. Today is my
birthday and I was really hoping I'd be back in New York by now. We're filming more reactions to the Mothership leaving. But so many extras have quit,
we can only shoot medium closeups. The Big Set looks almost empty. I'm
used to three or four hundred people milling around; only 100 are left. Even
Phil Dodds finally got to go back home.

The ETs are buying their back-to-school wardrobes, and Clark Paylow is
telling me we absolutely have to be finished here this week because the
company that owns the hangar has leased it to somebody else. I have heard
this before. I hope someone remembers it's my birthday. I drop a couple of
hints to the extras, thinking word will spread. So far it hasn't. I kept waiting
during lunch for someone to walk in with one of those big sheet cakes, but
we had jello for dessert. François and I were rushed to the set immediately
after lunch. Steven wants to film a closeup of us looking at the Mothership
as Richard gets into it. We will watch as it slowly closes, revs up its engine
and starts flying into space. A very dramatic moment. Actually, the
Mothership has done a lot of wonderful things these last weeks. Today, of
course, it's just sitting there, looking like the forty thousand pounds of steel
and black velvet that it is. I don't feel much like reacting to it.

Steven takes us aside for a quick huddle. François is to look enviously at
Richard as he enters the Mothership, and then watch affectionately and

wonderingly as the ship takes off into the universe. Steven wants me to cry. I have been thinking about this last shot since I arrived in Mobile. I have been dredging up sad moments from my life regularly, keeping them in shape for today. Actually, I don't have to do much reflecting or thinking or anything, because I really am sad it's going to be over soon. I never thought I could feel affection for the world's largest sauna bath, but the idea of not having the hangar to come to every day is very depressing. I will miss these people.

Steven begins to film, and François looks over at me, worried. I seem very unhappy. Steven dollies the camera in closer on François for a single, then back for our two-shot again. He starts to push in on me and he talks to me, softly. I am incredibly sad. Steven coaches us. He says that Richard has now entered the ship, and it's taking off. We start following it upwards with our eyes, and I hope François and I are watching it leave at the same speed, since there's nothing actually rising. I am playing 'When You Wish Upon A Star' over and over in my head, and it goes great with the picture. I remember how the man who did Jiminy Cricket's voice tried to date my aunt once. It's all going really well. As we watch the Mothership disappear, François is looking wistful and I look like somebody died. Steven yells "Cut!" and comes over to François and me to tell us how happy he is with the take. François asks if I'm all right — he is worried because I am crying. We film the same thing from different points of view: Richard walking into the ship and looking back at us; technicians from the back of the thinning crowd looking over at us; and the ETs looking up at us.

It's getting late, and I doubt I'll get home tonight. The last plane out of here is at seven. François and I are booked on it, but it's five o'clock and we haven't filmed Richard entering the ship yet. I find Clark again. He must really be getting sick of me. He says we will shoot tonight until we finish. We really do have to be out of here.

I go out to the kitchen to see if anyone's hiding a cake. The extra who gives me drawings finds me and gives me another drawing. It's a space creature with thousands of scales that he's obviously worked on for hours. I admire it, and put it in my briefcase with the twelve or thirteen other drawings he's already given me.

We go back to the set. Richard is padding around in his red satin space suit, adjusting his flight harness. He will enter the ship and its gravitational field will supposedly take effect and lift him up into the air.* Technicians practice raising and lowering him a couple of times, and Richard throws kisses to everybody. He likes being up there.

Steven rehearses the action a couple of times. Richard approaches the ship. The mylar bottom is in its 'down' position, and Richard is supposed to walk up it. He will be flown just as his head disappears into the ship. The feet on Richard's costume are very slippery, and every time he tries to walk up into the ship, he slides back down. Someone runs and gets rubber to put on the soles of his feet, and he rehearses some more. Steven is ready for a take. The fog machines start up, and Steven yells "Action!" Richard walks slowly up to the ship. He takes a last look to François. He looks over to Melinda and Cary. Steven instructs him to take one final look and realize he's leaving everything behind. He does, and then turns slowly to the Mothership. He walks up it a few feet and doesn't slip. His shoulders disappear up into the black body of the Mothership, and his feet begin to rise off the ground very slowly. He hovers for a moment, and then gently and very smoothly, glides up into the Mothership. The crane operators work the hydraulic lift and the whole bottom of the ship starts pulling up. The light streaming out of its silvery bottom gets dimmer, until only a thin line of bright white light remains. And then it closes up tight. Another machine starts to grind, and the whole Mothership starts rising out of frame. It is beautiful. Steven yells "Cut", and everything is lowered quickly so Dreyfuss can get out of the ship, which is, as usual, getting extremely hot. Dreyfuss emerges, sweating, and Steven shoots the scene a few more times. Steven thinks they started flying Richard a little early. He just wants to see the suggestion of flight.

We are almost through. Steven wants us to stay for one more reaction to the ETs' hand signals, and Julia's assistant comes to get me. She is probably going to tell me I have to work tomorrow.

She leads me upstairs to Julia's office. I enter and see a huge sheet cake with lots of candles and yellow roses sitting on Julia's desk. Julia and Kendall sing 'Happy Birthday'. I love it. I cut wedges to bring down to everybody, and eat a few pieces myself. An AD comes running after me. I have to do more reactions. I run downstairs with the cake, and François and I take our positions once more. Steven shoots very quickly and we're through with the coverage in about half an hour. We're finished. I have been trying to get out of this place for weeks and now it's all over. It's very hard to believe. I stand around for a minute, expecting someone to say we really have another few shots, and then I notice that everybody is actually leaving.

François is rushing to his office to change, and most of the extras have gotten out of their costumes and are getting into their cars. I run after François and say a very quick goodbye. We say we'll write. In a few minutes everybody but Steven and the camera crew have left, and I'm all alone in the front office, feeling totally abandoned. I have checked out of my hotel, thinking foolishly that we would finish early, and have no place to stay this evening. I sit around waiting for dailies to be over and ask Steven if I can stay at his house tonight.

Steven's cook is whipping up a fabulous Southern dish. Steven says dinner will have to wait because Mike Kahn wants to show him something. Steven asks if I'd like to watch too, and we go out to the porch where Michael has set up the editing equipment. I have not seen one frame of this movie since I watched Melinda try to pull Cary through the doggy door, so of course I say yes. Steven and Michael have completed editing the entire sequence in which the UFO makes its attack on Melinda's house. Michael wants to show Steven a chunk of it in which Melinda bumps into a stereo and it begins to play. When Steven filmed the scene he didn't record any music, and Michael and Steven have been trying to come up with just the right song to play during this section.

Michael threads the Movieola. We gather anxiously around to watch the scene. There is no sound to begin with, just Melinda's house in chaos. And then Melinda, carrying Cary, turns frantically and bumps into the record player. Michael presses a button, and 'Chances Are...' starts playing. He wants Steven to hear what it sounds like as background for the scene. Melinda runs into the kitchen as the refrigerator goes haywire and food falls out. 'Chances Are...' keeps going. The song is perfect because it's so incongruous. Steven is ecstatic. "Play it again, Michael," and we watch Melinda hurtle around her house three more times while Johnny Mathis sings.

I realize that I can't wait to see the whole thing put together. I don't think that will be for a very long time.

Spielberg shows Truffaut how three thousand Indian extras will point into the sky.

# INDIA

**MONDAY, SEPTEMBER 13**

Spoke to Lance today about when we will be going to India. Columbia is telling him the end of the month, too. We are both pretty doubtful.

Lance tells me he stayed in Mobile after filming on the Big Set was over. He says that after I left, Clark Paylow held an auction and sold everything in the hangar, except for what Steven needed in L.A. for additional shooting. He says Clark sold everything, down to every last papier-mache rock off Devil's Tower!

Big rocks were fifteen dollars. Little ones were eight.

**OCTOBER 1**

Truffaut sent Lynnie and me an invitation to the opening of *Small Change* at the New York Film Festival. Spent the week figuring out whether or not to buy a bow tie for my velvet suit.

We get to the theater early in the hopes of running into him, but he is probably waiting backstage. I hope he is nice to me when he sees me. I hope he remembers me. We get to our seats and read the program notes. Truffaut's two daughters have parts in the film, and I want to make sure I know who they are.

The lights go down, and Truffaut is introduced. The audience goes crazy. Truffaut looks embarrassed and very little down there on the stage. It reminds me of his scene in the auditorium with the hand signals. He speaks a few words in English and I can tell he has been working on this a long time, because his pronunciation is excellent. I catch myself checking out his grammar, and shake my head. Truffaut makes a joke about his English, segues into French, and talks about the film a little. And then the film begins.

After the movie, we go to a party at the Tavern-on-the-Green. A friend of Truffaut's comes up to me and says that Truffaut is here and has been looking for me. He was worried that I didn't come. He was worried that maybe I wouldn't like the film. He remembers me.

I see him over in a corner having his picture taken. He's really happy to see me. He says hello and turns me around to face the cameras. He tells me in French to make sure the photographers spell my name correctly.

Suddenly, it's like old times. I have a million things to say. We talk and laugh, and I tell him how much I love his movie. It's just like being in Mobile, except it's not 120 degrees and there aren't any fog machines.

We talk about India. We agree we'll never get there.

## OCTOBER 11

Got a telegram today from Julia Phillips: "Leaving for India end of the month. Get shots and arrange passport as quickly as possible." We're really going. I call Richard. He says he may be in India, too. Richard never finished his drive-bys in Mobile, and Julia is considering finishing them in India.

We will be going to the city of Benares. Evidently there is a religious festival there, and thousands of diseased Indians come to Benares to bathe their sins in the Ganges. Someone called it the Leper Festival. Steven wants to film François and me in this crowd. I hope they're not contagious. I hope we can get reservations at a good hotel. Do they *have* hotels in Benares?

I rush to get my yellow fever shot. I have a terrible reaction to it, and am in bed for two days.

Get another telegram from Julia: "Not going to India end of the month. Change in schedule. Will call with details."

She calls with details — we won't be going to India until January. I hope my vaccination lasts that long.

## JANUARY 5, 1977

Another call from Julia's office. We're not going to India this month. The effectiveness of my yellow fever vaccine is officially terminated.

I decide to stop leading my life with my bags packed, ready to go to India, and I have a major haircut. Practically a crew cut; I've been getting tired of *Close Encounter*'s hair.

## JANUARY 21

Julia's office calls again. We're going to India in February. To Bombay, though, not Benares. Apparently we're too late for the Leper Festival. *This* time it's definite, I'm told. Since I assume we're not really going, I don't bother to tell anybody that my hair is short and I've lost ten pounds.

I am not getting any more shots until I have my ticket in my hand.

## FEBRUARY 16

Columbia's travel department has booked me on a flight to Bombay. I now officially believe we're going to India. I will stop in London, Paris, Frankfurt and Kuwait, and the trip will take twenty-four hours. I call Air India to get some travel information and find out the price of my first-class ticket — almost $3000. I am stunned. I immediately decide to go tourist and pocket the difference. There is a cheaper way to go than tourist, but I would have to stay on in India for at least two weeks and I am not all that happy about being there for five days.

I begin calling around to find who at Columbia can help me trade in my ticket; a nice-sounding person in the travel department finally says he could probably help. He suggests that I come right over to his office to discuss the matter. I must bring my passport and some really good corned beef. Honest to God.

I happen to know where to get the world's best corned beef, so I run out and get ten bucks' worth and hurry over to Columbia. The receptionist sniffs in my direction a couple of times, but finally sends me to an inner office. The man inside asks me where the corned beef is, and then proceeds to tell me how to change my ticket. First he asks if the corned beef is very lean. He explains that it may be difficult to get Air India to give me money back for the ticket exchange, but he could probably pull some strings and get me some Air India tickets for the difference in price. He says that they're a little strange over at Air India. *They're* a little strange?

I go immediately to Air India to get my tourist ticket. I notice three or four ticket sellers and try to decide who looks the most accessible. I decide to try a gorgeous lady in a sari. She turns out to be extremely pleasant, but very aware of the rules. I cannot get any money back for downgrading my ticket, but the lady will arrange for me to get a credit in plane tickets. I tell her why I'm going to India. I ask if by any chance she knows my friend Reva who went recently to India to adopt a child. I know India is a big place, but why not ask? In fact, she does know Reva, and even knitted a pair of mittens for her baby. I consider this a real omen. I may not get yellow fever after all.

We complete the transaction and she gives me her brother's phone number in Delhi. I grab a bunch of exotic-looking folders as I start to leave. The lady reminds me to give her brother a call and I promise I will. I leave secure in the knowledge that I have at least one person to look up on my trip. Maybe I'll invite him to the set for lunch. I check out Delhi on my travel-folder map; it's about 900 miles north of Bombay.

## FEBRUARY 17

I get some more shots. My arms are killing me. Only a smallpox vaccination is legally required, but I'm terrified I'll pick up an incurable disease in Bombay, and have a series of shots for everything from typhus to cholera.

I tell my agent I'm worried about the facilities in Bombay, and ask him to get me the same dressing room arrangements as Truffaut. I figure if I don't have it in my contract, I'll be out there dressing with the water buffalo. Columbia says they can't guarantee this, and a two-week battle ensues. I hold my ground, and at last my demands are met — I will have the same dressing room in India as Truffaut. I am very relieved.

## FEBRUARY 20

I am sitting on Air India's Flight 135 on my way to Bombay, listening to Indian music and watching stewardesses in saris glide by. I've selected the American meal, realizing this will be the last food I trust for a week. We make a stop in London and I walk around Heathrow airport for a few minutes.

Then to Paris where Truffaut gets on with a reporter from *L'Express* and a photographer. It's great to see him. We tell jokes, have champagne, and feel like a family that's about to be reunited. I fall asleep for several hours, and I am awakened when the pilot points out Baghdad on the left. I expect to see flying carpets.

When we stop in Kuwait several sheiks wearing white robes over their business suits get on, and I realize I'm on the other side of the world.

## FEBRUARY 22

I left for India Sunday night at 8:30, but arrive today, Tuesday, at 5:30 in the morning. The airport is jammed and very disorganized. We are whisked through baggage claims by some local Columbia Pictures representatives, and as we leave the airport, leis of fresh flowers are thrown over our heads and we have an impromptu press conference. India has a huge film industry and the Indian press is thrilled to meet Truffaut, as several of his films have been shown in Bombay festivals. They have never heard of Steven Spielberg, since *Jaws* did not pass the government's strict censorship rules and was not shown in India.

We are driven from one side of Bombay to the other at breakneck speed through dirty, smelly, crowded streets. We get to the Taj Mahal Hotel, and are led past a horde of beggars into the lobby. The lobby is very crowded, and as I go to the check-in desk, I overhear a man talking. He has just returned from a walk outside the hotel. First he says, he noticed his watch missing. Then he felt into his pocket and couldn't find his wallet. He reached into his coat and discovered his key case was missing. Welcome to India.

We check in and are led to our rooms. The smell of incense and curry is everywhere, and a host of bag boys accompany us to the rooms. In the hallways an army of kids are cleaning the walls and floors. Then why does it look so dirty? I get to my room and fall immediately to sleep. I am awakened an hour later by a noise outside my window. An Indian worker is walking along the ledge of my fourth-floor window, painting the front of the hotel. Culture shock.

I go downstairs and join the camera crew for lunch. I study the menu intently, trying to avoid unpeeled fruits, raw vegetables and local water. I realize that there is not one item on the menu I would consider safe to eat. I finally decide to risk it with Spaghetti Bolognese. I figure everything in it is totally cooked, and it doesn't involve any vegetables. It arrives, covered with parsley, and since I don't know whether it's dried or fresh, I pick around the edges of the sauce, and eat a piece of bread. I don't know how long I will survive on bread and tomato sauce. I order bottled water, but it arrives with the cap half-off, and has "Bottled in India" written all over it, so I don't drink it.

The sound man tells me a story about a religious colony near the hotel which keeps their dead on big tables behind their apartment complex. The bodies dry in the sun like raisins, and the vultures come and carry the bones away. Sometimes they drop things as they fly. He tells me to watch for falling digits. He may be saying this to frighten me.

I make a foray outside of the hotel. I have a wad of one-dollar bills with which to bargain with the natives, as I have heard you can get some really good deals if you're carrying small American bills. There are some fascinating shops behind the hotel. I stop in a small jewelry store next to a crumbling arcade, and have to brush away an ancient-looking wool carpet to enter. Very quaint. When I get inside a big sign on the wall says "We Accept American Express Credit Cards." I try to bargain with my dollars and no one wants to (a) bargain; or (b) take my American money. So I have to stop back at the hotel to get rupees. I buy some ivory bracelets and a jade key ring. Someone actually comes up to me on the street and asks if I want to buy "Feelthy Postcards".

Later at the hotel, Spielberg explains the India filming to Truffaut and me. We will be shooting two hours outside of Bombay in a primitive village called Hal. Truffaut and I have come to the village with our crew of scientists to investigate a UFO sighting. We will mingle with three thousand local villagers who have been recruited to play three thousand local villagers, record their five-note chant and try to find out what has really gone on. All that we're waiting for now is the camera which has not been released from Customs. The Customs officials think that Columbia Pictures is sending in cameras to sell, and Columbia is doing their best to convince the officials they are only using them to film a movie.

I confess to Spielberg how ridiculous I'm being about the food and water, and he tells me he's been taping a Band Aid over his mouth when he washes his face to prevent water from touching his lips. I hadn't thought of that.

At dinner tonight, Julia Phillips comes over to my table.

She's very concerned because she has heard I'm refusing to eat or drink anything. She says I will start fainting. I order a Coke and drink it, even though, like the water, it says "Bottled in Bombay". Julia asks me if I have been taking my malaria pills. She and Spielberg have been on theirs for several weeks already. My doctor never mentioned them. I try not to panic.

Julia says she and Spielberg drove through the red-light district today and saw women being sold from wooden cages. Some people reached into her car and grabbed at her, and she said it was truly horrifying. Spielberg asks if I want to go see it with him tomorrow, and I decide not to.

This India sequence which seems so extravagant is actually costing Columbia very little. Julia explains that when Columbia exhibits movies in India their profits cannot be taken from the country but are kept 'frozen' in rupees in local banks, and much of this sequence is being paid for out of this money.

There are a lot of people dressed like Lawrence of Arabia in the lobby. An Iranian sheik tells me that Bombay in February is very "in" this year. You couldn't have told that from me.

At lunch today I tell François that Lynnie and I are having a baby in the Fall. He's really excited. He starts calling me "little father". He hopes it's a girl. The waiter comes over and I order my fourth bowl of Spaghetti Bolognese, and ask them to hold the parsley. I tell them I am allergic to parsley. "Please," I say, "no parsley."

They give me parsley. Truffaut laughs at me and tells me I shouldn't worry about the food, it's fine. I say that I don't believe him. He tells me that when his daughters were little they never believed him, either. He was always telling them that the word for "hat" was "shoe", or he'd point to a lamp and say "saltshaker". He says that one day it was raining very hard, so he told them they had better wear raincoats and take their umbrellas. They laughed and rushed out with no coats, assuming it was a sunny day.

**FEBRUARY 24**

Our cars pick us up at 5:00 A.M. and we start the two-hour trip to Hal. At last we work. Truffaut and I are terrified of our driver, who appears to be a madman. I explain to him that we don't care if we're a little late, but he still insists on driving on the wrong side of the road to "avoid traffic". We finally reach an arid stretch of rocks, hills and scruff, surrounded by some crumbling buildings and a lot of mosquitoes. This is our location.

I ask an assistant director for directions to Truffaut's and my dressing rooms. He points to a few empty camera boxes near a large leafless tree. For this my agent fought for two weeks? We spend most of the day sitting on our boxes, trying unsuccessfully to avoid the scorching sun and a couple of nearby water buffalo.

After a lunch of warm pieces of unidentifiable meat that have been wrapped in paper and left sitting in the sun for as long as we have, Truffaut and I are called to rehearse. We are to run up a small hill through thousands of extras who sit chanting.

We rehearse five or six times, and while it's hard for us to repeat our path through the sea of three thousand Indians, it is even harder for the camera crew to accomplish their complicated dolly shot. We begin shooting the scene, and repeat our action seven or eight times. In the middle of one take, Truffaut stops halfway up the hill and starts to pass out. His eyes are glassy, he is breathing hard, he can hardly speak. He looks like he's having a heart attack, and two assistant directors carry him into a tent and start applying ice to his pressure points. He finally catches his breath and says he thinks it's just the heat. He is driven fifteen miles to the nearest bathroom, returns an hour later still looking shaken, and we continue shooting the scene.

Steven has hired a local Indian choral leader to stand on a hill and lead the three thousand extras in the famous five notes with which we will eventually communicate with the Mothership. Take after take, the leader sings the wrong five notes. ADs rush over to him and sing the correct ones in his ears. Unfortunately, they keep giving him the wrong notes. He gets upset. He is carrying a religious prayer gourd, and as the cameras reload he removes a pair of thick eyeglasses and a pack of Camels from it. He lights up and nervously studies his music. Filming begins, and he stuffs everything back into the gourd. He never does get the notes right, and all three thousand extras spend several hours following him in the incorrect response.

We're falling behind schedule. Many of the extras are religious Moslems, and during their lunch break they have gone to pray at a nearby mosque. They straggle back to work a couple of hours later.

We spend another hour trying to get a horde of natives to point straight up to the sky and yell. Take after take, one native points his finger in the wrong direction, or another takes his hand down before Steven is finished filming.

Later, Spielberg positions Truffaut and me on top of a large hill and instructs the extras to run towards us when he yells "action". He rehearses the crowd a few times, and everything goes without a hitch. The cameras are positioned, Traffaut and I take our places, and Spielberg yells "action".

The cameras roll and the three thousand extras make a mad dash — in the wrong direction, away from the cameras, hungrily chasing an emaciated rabbit. The chase continues for several hundred yards, until the rabbit disappears down a hole. The extras return to their start marks and we get the shot in the first take.

Later, Truffaut and I film our entrance. We drive down a dirt road jammed with extras, hit a mark, and jump out of the car. We rehearse the scene a number of times and then start to film it. It's difficult to hit our mark because the extras keep walking over it, so we have to do a great number of takes. To amuse ourselves, we tell each other jokes. I tell a very silly, old story about a conversation overheard in the balcony of a movie theater. The punchline is "You pee on my date and you're *sorry?*" We're both pretty slap-happy at this point, and Truffaut thinks this is the funniest thing he has ever heard. He laughs so hard that I start laughing too. Spielberg yells "action", and we drive down the dirt road laughing so hard we're almost crying. Truffaut gets out of the car trying to hide a big smile. For the rest of the day, whenever Truffaut looks at me he starts to laugh.

## SATURDAY, FEBURARY 26

I'm going back to N.Y.C. tonight. I pack up my ivory and Tibetan painting I bought, and I decide to leave behind my Gucci loafers which are caked in two days' worth of Indian dirt. Years from today people will wonder why the hallman at the Taj is wearing $80 loafers.

I go to the lobby to say goodbye to everybody. Truffaut has just bought ivory bracelets for his daughters, Julia Phillips is trying to decide whether to buy an Oriental rug, and Spielberg is in the gift shop buying souvenirs. He selects a mahogany Taj Mahal whose turrets pull out to become steak knives, and a mahogany fish whose fins pull off to become steak knives. He says he will sterilize them when he gets back to L.A. and hopes the fins and turrets don't come apart.

I leave for the airport, and it doesn't really hit me until I'm over Paris that I may never see any of these people again.

Dreyfuss enters the Mothership in the 'Special Edition'. This was shot *post* post-production.

# POST-PRODUCTION

It's May. I'm going back to NYU part-time to get the degree I never completed nine years ago. I've heard some rumors about additional filming, but I think they're unfounded.

## MAY 6

I get a call that Spielberg wants to do some additional filming. Hopefully he will wait until I complete my courses. I call Spielberg and he says he hasn't decided where to film yet, but Columbia executives have screened a rough cut and are so excited about the picture they have given Spielberg the money to film whatever additional scenes he wants. He says Truffaut and I will refilm our introduction in the film. Spielberg says our "dirty book" scene at the airport was too static, and we will film another one that will now open the movie. He says we will probably film in the Brazilian jungle. I will be paddling down the Amazon in a canoe. Giant bugs will be crawling up my legs. I will come upon Truffaut as he tries to talk with some natives in a clearing filled with World War II airplanes. I ask if they will be real or prop bugs.

## MAY 14

On the plane to L.A. for additional shooting. I have missed my final exams. François and I will be filming our new introduction in the Mojave Desert a couple of hours outside L.A., instead of in a Brazilian jungle. I'm relieved. We're also adding a scene in a radio control room in which I will discover that the numbers the Mothership has been broadcasting are really the longitude and latitude of Devil's Tower.

The costume man called me last night, hysterical. Steven has decided to do more closeups of our reactions to the ETs. We must wear the same clothes we were wearing last year when we filmed the sequence. I took my wardrobe home last year and lost the tie I had been wearing in that scene. As I fly over the Grand Canyon, there is a man in L.A. frantically searching for a ten year-old seersucker tie.

## MAY 17

Working in the Mojave Desert today. The limousine picked me up at five this morning. We called for Truffaut at his hotel, and started north on the freeway. Truffaut and I are exhausted. We sleep for part of the trip and ask our driver questions for the rest. Ranch-style houses give way to one-room shacks, and it starts to look like desert outside the car window. The driver explains that people bought land out here a long time ago, thinking that the area would become as developed as the San Fernando Valley. The irrigation systems never worked out, and now they are stuck with worthless pieces of arid desert property. As he speaks, he takes out the map to the location and stares at it intently. He should talk less and drive more.

He pulls off the road. I ask if we are lost. Of course not, he says, he has followed directions perfectly and we are here. There is clearly no one else within five miles of this deserted plateau, and I suggest we try to find a phone somewhere and call the studio to find out where everybody is. We backtrack a couple of miles and find a little shack. The guy inside tells us he knows where the movie is filming, and we follow him up two miles of winding dirt road to the location. We could never in a million years have found it ourselves.

The honeywagons are all set up, and remnants of a decaying Mexican village have been erected in the middle of a vast dry lake. It's a gorgeous day, absolutely no wind, and I wonder what Spielberg has in mind, because in the script it says "blinding dust storm". I look to the left and see seven or eight giant wind machines standing next to a large generator. Bags of Fuller's Earth are piled nearby. It's going to be a hard day.

I examine the set: a rickety fence leads to an adobe shack that bears a sign, 'Drink Coca Cola'. An animal trainer is tending his burros who have just ambled out of their animal trailer and are trying in vain to find something to graze on. Behind the shack, fifteen World War II fighter planes are lined up, and I go over to inspect them. The script refers to them as "in brand new condition", and they really are. They were flown in last night, and have been polished and shined all morning. They have girls' names painted on their sides, and their underbellies are decorated with WWII insignia. I expect to see John Hodiak in one of the cockpits.

I go to my trailer to put on my costume. It's freezing out here. By the time I emerge wearing my combat boots and green Army hat the special effects people are showing Spielberg the wind effect. One man operates each giant wind machine, and two or three others cluster around him holding bags of Fuller's Earth which they gradually empty into the path of the whirring blades. The effect produces everything from clouds of dust to a blinding sandstorm, depending upon the speed of the fans and the force with which the bag-holders hurl the dirt. I wonder if it can be healthy to breathe all this dust, but the set designer explains there is absolutely nothing to worry about. Then why, I ask myself, are Steven and the entire crew wearing goggles and gas masks?

Filming begins. Truffaut and his outfit drive up to the shack. An Army officer emerges from the dust storm. The action is rehearsed a few times, then Spielberg calls for a final runthrough with wind. The fans start up and the dust starts blowing, and I step back about fifty feet because it is impossible to see or breathe anywhere near the scene. The man getting out of the car can't find where he is going, and walks away from the camera. The focus puller can't see anything to focus on. Spielberg yells "Cut the wind", but no one can hear him because the fans make so much noise. Finally, one of the fan operators realizes the scene must be over by now and cuts his machine. The others get the idea, and the storm comes to an abrupt halt. Everyone takes a few minutes to brush off the dust, and the makeup man rushes about with Kleenex for people to wipe their eyes and blow their noses. The crew and cast reassemble and Spielberg yells "Action!" once more. The take goes smoothly, except that the wind machines focused towards the background are not sending out enough dust, and this makes the dust storm in the foreground look unreal. Finally they get the right combination, Spielberg yells "Print", and the machines grind to a halt.

I look over at Charlsie, the script lady. She has never budged from her canvas chair behind the camera all during the storm and I wonder how she has survived. She looks like the Invisible Woman. She wears gloves and has wrapped her head in a large bandanna. Her sunglasses stick out from beneath a large canvas hat, and her master script is covered in a layer of heavy cellophane. This lady knows how to take care of herself on location.

It's a clear desert day. I can see snow-capped mountains miles in the distance. I hear a plane's engine, and look up and see a glider getting a lift upwards. The towplane pulls it up to about two thousand feet and suddenly the connecting wire is dropped and the glider is released. I watch the glider float silently for a couple of minutes. It's all very idyllic. Then a roar of engines and a dense cloud of Fuller's Earth hits me in the face, and I remember why we are here.

There's an old Mexican man sitting near the makeup wagon. He's wearing beat up overalls, and half of his face looks like he's had acid thrown all over it. The makeup man is applying rubbery goo to make it look as if the skin were peeling away, and Spielberg runs over for a minute to check the guy out. "More burn, less red." And then he's back to the dustbowl. I introduce myself to the man, and he is charming. He turns out to be a former opera singer and oldtime movie actor. He speaks four languages. We say a few words in French, and I can't wait to introduce him to Truffaut. He'll love this guy. As I turn to leave, the man asks if I like opera, and he starts to sing an aria in German, making wildly dramatic gestures. I am transfixed by the sight of this sweet old man with burn makeup all over his face, singing his heart out in the middle of the Mojave Desert.

We finally break for the traditional location lunch of rectangular brown meat and lumpy gravy, and look over at the dirt-encrusted people who have been working all morning. Spielberg comes over to say hello and tells Truffaut and me that he has a great idea for the end of the scene which we'll be doing tomorrow. He has boundless energy, as usual. He jumps around from table to table making arrangements for tomorrow's lineup.

I'm in the next shot. I will be stationed in an official-looking Jeep about half a mile up the road, together with five or six extras in Army uniforms. When Spielberg gives the signal, we are to drive forward to a mark somewhere near where Truffaut's car has stopped. We rehearse. There is a problem. With the dust effect, the driver can neither see the stop mark, nor see Spielberg giving the signal to start. Finally, an AD sticks a walkie-talkie in the car and we wait for our signal. For three hours we drive forward, miss our mark in the whirling dust, and drive back again to starting position. At last we arrive speedily enough and hit the right mark, and we are on to the next set-up.

In the next shot I will be introduced to Truffaut. I've done this before. The words are the same, only the location is changed. Actually, this time the words are a little different. Since we finished principal photography last September the movie has been assembled, and Spielberg has decided to clue the audience in a little more to what's going on, right at the top of the film. He has also changed my profession. Last year I was a crackerjack interpreter. This year I yell to Truffaut over the wind machines that I am really a cartographer, but I happen to speak French. I figure Spielberg's protecting himself in case my linguistic efforts aren't convincing. "Well, he's not really an interpreter by profession, he's just helping out." I think of all the ways I could have acted more like a cartographer during last year's filming, if I had only known.

We shoot closeups now, and I am off-camera yelling at Truffaut. We spoke our first lines together almost a year and a half ago in Gillette, Wyoming, and I flash on how tense and scared we were then. Truffaut was worried about his English and I was hysterical about my French, and we really had to struggle to get through some of those scenes. It's different now. As I give my lines off-camera, Truffaut smiles a little, listening intently, amused by my character's efforts to explain himself, or more, perhaps, by the sight of old Balaban trying not to get blown over by the wind machines. He smiles when I do my line congratulating him for the great work he did in the breakthrough of '73, and when the wind machine actually pushes me over, he laughs. Spielberg yells "Cut!" It's a great take, and we reverse everything to do my closeup.

This time Truffaut is off-camera, and as soon as Spielberg yells "Action", he leans forward. He's really helping me. He's even funnier off-camera, and

I keep resisting the urge to break into a grin. Spielberg increases the wind at one point, and I trip for a second and have to re-position myself. Spielberg tells me after the take that it's his favorite thing I did today.

The crew moves over to the airplanes to set up. In the next shots, Truffaut and I investigate these planes. There are some technical difficulties getting the engines revved up at the right time, but basically everything is going smoothly. The old man comes over to chat with Truffaut, and as I guessed, Truffaut loves him. They reminisce about great old places in Paris.

We shoot a scene where we look in one of the cockpits and realize that these planes have just landed. There is no rational explanation of how the planes got here, or why they are in such good condition, and I must back up yelling things like, "How?" and "Why?" As I back up, the camera must move with me. I also have to increase the intensity of my questioning. The guy in the cockpit must also get his foot to a new position by my second line. By the time we get all this right in the same take, the sun is setting.

We drive back to a local motel and do our best to clean up for dinner. I eat with some of the ADs, and we talk about the germs in India and how hot it was in Mobile. Michael Phillips joins us. I've only seen him twice since filming began. He and Julia Phillips are producing the movie together, he explains, but they do most of their work as a team during pre-production. While the movie is actually filming, only one of them stays in touch with day-to-day operations because more than one boss is confusing. That sounds sensible to me. He says the movie is looking great, and when I ask if I should buy Columbia stock, Michael says it's a good idea. He had been at the shooting all day today, but I never saw him through all the dust. We promise to say hello to each other tomorrow.

## MAY 18

Working with the old man today. He sits in front of the adobe shack and mumbles something in Spanish. Spielberg asks him if he can cry, and the man immediately bursts into tears. There is a lot of setting up, so I stand off-camera and find Michael Phillips near some Fuller's Earth bags. It's a good thing we found each other at the beginning of the day — after the dust storm, he probably wouldn't recognize me.

Spielberg and I talk about how wonderful the old man is. Spielberg loves the way he talks, and does an imitation of him that is uncanny, with a husky voice, Spanish accent and all. He even looks up sadly as he does it. I tell Spielberg that if the man isn't available for looping, he could do his voice and no one would know. Spielberg says it's not a bad idea.

Spielberg describes the next shot and we rehearse it briefly. In it, I will back up slowly and look up at the sky wonderingly. As I do this, the dust will get thicker and thicker, and, finally, I will disappear. The crew has to relight as it is the end of the day. Someone says we'd better hurry, because the light in the desert goes quickly.

Everything is in position, and I go over to do my big walk backwards. The camera's dolly tracks have been laid down right where I'm supposed to be backing up. I rehearse the shot. I translate my line: "The sun came out last night and sang to us" for Truffaut, and then back up slowly. My feet can't find a path between the wooden tracks, and I am unable to move without falling. I practice walking backwards a couple of times, and finally work out a way to avoid the tracks and still reach my mark in time. I look like a crippled geisha girl. More practice, and finally there I am, walking backwards and looking up at the sky. The camera is rolling, and clouds of dust are billowing around me. My foot touches my mark and I stop. I even remember not to look at my foot. I raise my eyes towards the sky. I tilt my head backwards. Spielberg yells, "Perfect!" I scan the sky tentatively; Spielberg calls out for more Fuller's Earth, and I am totally obliterated in a blinding storm of stinging dust. Spielberg yells, "Cut! Print!" The wind halts, the dust settles, and I am caked with dirt from head to foot. My beard is so filled with dust I look like Santa Claus.

I can't wait to go home.

**MAY 19**

We're filming today on a soundstage at The Burbank Studios. Truffaut and I go to makeup, and I have my bald spot drawn in again. This year it takes longer.

I get into the same costume I wore in Mobile last year. Same shirt, same tie, same awful shoes. It's a weird feeling. The prop man brings my briefcase out for me. It's like seeing an old friend. Instinctively, I reach for it with my left hand, and I feel the remnants of my old callouses press against the handle.

Truffaut and I start onto the stage. A guard stops us. He explains that this is a closed set and he cannot allow us on. I tell him we're in the movie. He doesn't believe us. We have to find an AD to clear us.

Heard from Steven that a guy has been going around Florida pretending to be Dreyfuss. Dreyfuss says that someone has been passing bad checks using his name and, as Dreyfuss, has gotten engaged to a country club owner's daughter. Dreyfuss has actually seen pictures of him in the local paper and says he does look a little bit like him. The guy even gives interviews as Richard. He makes up things about Richard's life. He talks about how he went to the Pasadena Playhouse, which Richard didn't, and how he had to gain a lot of weight for a part in a movie and is having trouble losing it, which is also not true. I begin to think that you haven't really made it unless you have an imposter, and wish that I had one. And then I realize that many people think I am an imposter.

Steven has had a mechanical ET constructed. It's on the set now, and he's terrified that someone will sneak in and take a picture of it. Before *Jaws* was released, someone got hold of a photograph of the shark, and Steven doesn't want to get scooped again.

Steven is talking with William Fraker, who's filming the additional L.A. sequences. They are trying to figure out where to place the camera in the crowded module that rests against the back wall. It's a problem. The module is jam-packed with machinery, and there's hardly any room for the actors in the scene. They decide to shoot from outside the module, and the crew re-positions the camera.

Steven comes over to talk to us. We go over the new scene. I just got the pages, and I've had a hard time memorizing the extremely technical jargon. I have written my lines on a piece of paper which I hold in my hand and refer to as frequently as possible. The scene will begin with Truffaut and me at a computer console. Truffaut will listen to a headset, while I casually watch the print-out. This is the scene when I break the code and discover the coordinates that bring us to Devil's Tower.

We get ready for the first shot. We are jammed into the module, and with the lights on it's almost like being back in Mobile. Truffaut kids around with his headset. "Its for you," he says, handing it to me. Meanwhile, sound people are reaching up our pants legs, wiring us with antennae and microphones, and making standard jokes about hoping they don't damage anything. I look at my piece of paper and wonder if I'll be able to learn my lines before we start shooting.

While Stephen shoots coverage of the scientists in the module, François and I catch up on news. He's going to be spending the summer in L.A. because he's got a three-picture deal with Roger Corman. His daughters will be joining him, so he's got to look for a house to rent. Truffaut says his daughters love Los Angeles, and that they speak wonderful English. They are crazy about the Beatles and learned English by listening to their albums over and over. I ask how *The Man Who Loved Women* turned out, and he says he likes it a lot.

We break for lunch and go to the commissary. We're sitting there having our fairly stale roast beef sandwiches, when the American producer of *Day for Night* comes over to say hello. François is very happy to see him. François says that Columbia had the original deal with him on *Day for Night*, but when they saw the script they decided that people do not want to see a movie about moviemaking.

Truffaut talks about his next movie. It's about death, and he's writing it himself. It is based on several Henry James short stories, and Truffaut has budgeted it lower than his usual $800,000 a picture. This one will be done for $500,000, because he figures movies about death don't make a lot of money. He says that after his experiences on *Close Encounters* he would really love to do another movie about making a movie. We start back to the set. They let us in this time, and we get back into our module.

We start with my closeup. I am to tear off the computer print-out and carry a piece of it with me. After a few rehearsals, there isn't much printed tape left, so I start taping pieces together and using the same one over again. The prop crew is greatly relieved. So am I, since I've written one of my more difficult lines on the back of the tape.

During a break, a crew member leads me to an office set and points to an oddly-shaped computer. He explains that it is used in high-priority security systems to prevent unauthorized personnel from entering a restricted area. We will be using the machine in the next shot,* so he wants me to become familiar with it. I press my hand onto a molded steel plate in the center of the machine. He lowers a pad over my fingers, and I hear a low, buzzing sound. He instructs me to press hard with the tips of my fingers. I repeat this process five times. Each time a new piece of information is recorded. The machine now has on file my fingerprints, the length of my fingers, the width of the spaces between them, the position of my knuckles, and the outline of my hand. It could make me a terrific pair of gloves.

Spielberg is talking with Carlo Rambaldi, the man who made King Kong and the mechanical ET that will work tomorrow. Spielberg wasn't happy with the way the Mobile ETs looked in closeup, so he's re-filming all of the closeups with Rambaldi's elaborate creation. Rambaldi looks more like a businessman than an inventor of movable monsters. He gestures animatedly, and spouts rapid Italian to Steven while his poor interpreter tries to keep up. I know how he feels. It seems there is a slight problem with the ET's cheek movements, and Rambaldi is concerned that everything will not go perfectly tomorrow. Spielberg assures him that it will.

## MAY 20

We're back at The Burbank Studios for what everybody says is our last day of filming. We're reacting to the ETs for one last time. I hope.

Carlo Rambaldi's mechanical ET is hidden under a canvas sheet, more for the purposes of secrecy than safety. Guards are everywhere.

Spielberg says he's going to let us all have a look at the little creature, and he leads us over to it like a proud father. He removes the covering to reveal a rubbery-looking four-foot figure standing frozen on its base. The figure is connected to dozens of levers lined up about ten feet away. Operators take their positions behind the levers, and as Spielberg gives commands, they start furiously pushing and pulling. The figure smiles, blinks its eyes, cocks its head and raises its arm to greet us. One lever operates a bellows in its chest that simulates breathing, and another makes its Adam's apple bob up and down. When it smiles, its mouth doesn't just turn up, its eyes narrow and several different cheek muscles contract. It's miraculous. I can almost forget the groaning of the levers and believe the thing is real.

There's a wrap party at the back of the set, but everyone hurries home to try to beat the rush hour. I grab a quick glass of champagne, change out of my costume and leave.

We've said a lot of goodbyes during the filming of this movie. It's hard to believe that this one is final.


**MAY 25**


I have to do some looping, re-recording bits of dialogue from the movie. I'm recovering from a terrible cold I caught in the Mojave Desert, and everytime I start to talk, I sneeze. My entire performance may take on a new nasal dimension.

Since I only see tiny snips of the film, I can't really tell how the movie looks. Dreyfuss told me that during his looping Spielberg had put in some of the special effects, but he hadn't wanted him to see them so he covered the top part of the screen where the effect was with a piece of black cardboard. Dreyfuss begged Steven to show him just one effect, so Stephen took the cardboard down, and Dreyfuss watched a UFO come zooming over his head. He screamed and almost fell out of his chair, he said, and he wished to God he could have seen this while he was in Mobile all those months looking up at the sky at... NOTHING!

I leave the studio and drive on the Ventura Freeway towards Benedict Canyon. Is it really over? Or will I be getting another call from Steven Spielberg next month telling me to pack for Australia. Or Africa. Or Outer Mongolia.

I could believe it. I could believe anything, now. I have watched an extra-terrestrial come to life, and climbed the hills of India with François Truffaut.

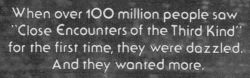

When over 100 million people saw
"Close Encounters of the Third Kind"
for the first time, they were dazzled.
And they wanted more.
NOW THERE IS MORE.

Director Steven Spielberg has filmed
additional scenes, designed to expand
the total experience of the original film.

NOW, FOR THE FIRST TIME,
FILMGOERS WILL BE ABLE TO SHARE
THE ULTIMATE EXPERIENCE
OF BEING *INSIDE*.

*Coming THIS SUMMER*

THE SPECIAL EDITION

# CLOSE ENCOUNTERS
OF THE THIRD KIND

A COLUMBIA/EMI Presentation
CLOSE ENCOUNTERS OF THE THIRD KIND
A PHILLIPS Production A STEVEN SPIELBERG Film
Starring RICHARD DREYFUSS also starring TERI GARR and MELINDA DILLON
with FRANCOIS TRUFFAUT as Lacombe
Music by JOHN WILLIAMS Visual Effects by DOUGLAS TRUMBULL
Director of Photography VILMOS ZSIGMOND, A.S.C. Produced by JULIA PHILLIPS
and MICHAEL PHILLIPS Written and Directed by STEVEN SPIELBERG

Read the Dell Book | Original Soundtrack Available | DOLBY STEREO | PG PARENTAL GUIDANCE SUGGESTED
Panavision® | On Arista Records And Tapes. | IN SELECTED THEATRES | SOME MATERIAL MAY NOT BE SUITABLE FOR CHILDREN

# EPILOGUE

## SUNDAY, OCTOBER 30, 1977

I'm seeing a screening of the movie for the first time tonight and I'm really nervous. The opening kept getting postponed because Spielberg was changing things. Small things: an added closeup of a Jiminy Cricket figurine in Richard Dreyfuss' den, inserts of hands opening doors, things like that.

Pulling up to the theater my heart starts to pound. The screenings tonight are for Columbia brass and the critics who have already had their junket to L.A. cancelled when the first opening date was postponed. They are probably arriving with loaded guns. The film is opening six months later than predicted, and came in nine million dollars over budget. And there is some fear that *Star Wars* may have stolen its thunder.

Columbia's campaign of secrecy before the movie's opening has begun to backfire, and the press is getting a little hostile. *New York Magazine* sneaked someone into a Dallas preview and has printed a rotten review. Columbia stock dropped so quickly that trading had to be stopped. *US Magazine* has been begging me to tell them about the movie, but I am sworn to secrecy. They are trying to find out what song is played at the end of the film. It feels like something out of Watergate. Phone conversation: "Is it a song from a children's movie? Don't answer if the answer is 'yes'. If it's 'no' keep talking." A tabloid has been trying to get me to do an interview for a cover story they are planning, and I call Spielberg to ask if I should do it. He tells me I shouldn't, but not to worry — they'll just make it up anyway.

A cab pulls up to the Ziegfeld Theater and autograph hounds are anxiously waiting. A few of them run over to me and ask for my autograph. They of course think I'm Dreyfuss. I say to myself that after tonight everybody will know I am not Dreyfuss. After all, there we'll be up on the screen together at the same time without trick photography. Once and for all the world will see that I am me and he is he. So for the last time, I sign Richard Dreyfuss' name in an autograph book

I present my hand-delivered, beautifully designed invitation to a man at the door, and as we walk through the crowds in the lobby it's beginning to dawn on me that I'm actually going to be in a movie. All those months in Mobile and Gillette are going to be up there on the screen for the next two hours, and it's very exciting. I say hello to Julia Phillips. She looks nervous, but we joke about how this is finally the night, and reminisce for a minute about her undulating fever in Bombay. I wish us all luck and look around for Spielberg. I figure he's hiding in the back of the theater somewhere. The theater is jammed, but we manage to find a pair of seats in the fifth row. Some friends of mine tap me on the shoulder, and as I turn to say hello, "Dreyfuss is here!" murmuring starts up. It's a good thing I like him so much.

The lights dim. The titles come on, and people applaud. There is a blinding flash, and a thunderous clap of music; at that moment you can feel the audience getting hooked. There's a great feeling of relief in the theater — Spielberg's done it again.

I watch the movie in a daze. I don't even mind how I look. Actually, I love the way I look. My God. Here and there a scene is cut, but that seems to help the build of the movie. The scene where the UFO passes Richard's truck is over, and the audience applauds wildly. Soon the Mothership appears. It looks nothing like the stills Steven kept showing us during filming. The Mothership I had pictured was a very dark hulk with some flashing lights, and what I'm looking at is a spectacular city of lights. Things I pretended to be looking at for months in Mobile are flashing by for real, this time, and I can't get over the fact that it really works. All those "look to the left and be surprised"s are paying off. Truffaut goes over to put his hand up to a hovering flying object and the look of wonderment that took Spielberg so many takes to get exactly right, is exactly right. And when Truffaut finally does his hand signals to Carlo Rambaldi's lone figure, I can hear sniffling all around us.

I had no idea the movie would have this effect on people. Spielberg kept telling us during the filming that the movie was very gentle; he wanted it to feel like an embrace.

As the Mothership takes off and the closing music begins, I anticipate Ukelele Ike's 'When You Wish Upon A Star', but Steven has cut it. He explains later that he got a lot of unfavorable comments about the song at the preview of the film in Dallas. The Mothership disappears into the distance, and the applause starts. Spielberg and the Columbia brass must be thrilled. I am. As we get up to leave the guy sitting next to us leans over to congratulate me. "Richard," he says, "You were great."

As we leave the theater I notice a limousine parked in front. Teri and Melinda are sitting in the back looking uncomfortable. I tap on the window and the chauffeur looks at me menacingly, but Teri waves me into the backseat. I ask where Steven is. They tell me he was too scared to come to the preview, and is waiting at his hotel for the whole thing to be over. Teri and Melinda have been nervous about the screening, too. Teri says she was in her suite at the Sherry, and the lights at her dressing table kept blinking on and off. Melinda thought that maybe this was a UFO contacting Teri. For tickets to the screening?

We call Spielberg at the hotel and tell him how great we think the movie is, and better, how much the audience liked it tonight. He's tremendously pleased, and says he will join us for a celebration drink at Elaine's.

Steven meets us at Elaine's with his girlfriend Amy Irving, and some friends. I ask Steven if François has seen the movie, and he says he saw it in L.A. and loved it. He was especially impressed by the fact that there were no bad guys in it.

François was the guest of honor at a special screening for Japanese distributors. Steven says he took one look at the Oriental interpreter Columbia had provided for the occasion, smiled and said, "Ah... Bob Balaban."

That makes me very happy.

**Miscellany:**

... I had to have a check okayed at my bank today, and an officer recognized me. A strange look came over his face and he asked if I was an actor. I said *"Close Encounters..."* He said it's his favorite movie, he's seen it four times, and he'll okay any check I bring him. He hopes I'm not embarrassed, but he wants to introduce me to a teller who has seen the movie eight times. He puts his initial on my check and leads me to the front of a line of forty people.

---

... Went to Philadelphia the other day to do a talk show about the movie. I was on a panel with a planetarium supervisor, a UFO investigator, and a lady who said she'd visited Venus. Interesting note: several respectable people in the audience told stories about having their cars followed by disc-like objects. It's like a scene from the movie.

---

... I'm at home watching TV and suddenly the commercial for *Close Encounters* comes on. There's Richard being shaken in his truck. There's the long road leading to the stars that's the logo for the movie. And suddenly, there I am, walking towards the camera, looking at the sky. I keep watching TV and see myself three more times in the next two hours. Saturation. Gene Shalit's review calls the movie one of the most spectacular films ever made. On *The Tonight Show*, Johnny Carson jokes about a "Close Encounter of the Worst Kind." A friend of mine calls to read me a cartoon in the *Los Angeles Times*: Begin and Sadat are pictured together at a conference table. The caption reads, "Close Encounters of the Fourth Kind." The impact of the movie is beginning to hit me. I feel like I'm part of history.

WIDESCREEN

A STEVEN SPIELBERG FILM

CLOSE
ENCOUNTERS
OF THE THIRD KIND
COLLECTOR'S
EDITION

COLUMBIA TRISTAR
HOME ENTERTAINMENT

WE ARE NOT ALONE

DVD
VIDEO
COMPATIBLE WITH
PlayStation 2

# LOOKING BACK

## WEDNESDAY, DECEMBER 5, 2001

It's been nearly twenty-five years since *Close Encounters* entered the upper stratosphere of cinema legendry, capturing the hearts and minds of millions of viewers. It broke box office records, and remains one of the most successful movies of all time. In 1980, the 'Special Edition' version of the film filled theaters all over again, and now there's the definitive DVD (which, incidentally, includes some of the deleted scenes I mention in the diary). I look back on it all now with a quarter century of perspective, and realize that nothing much has changed.

*Close Encounters* was always a great story, told in a compelling and magical way. And somehow, along with the special effects and the stirring music and his brilliant mastery of film technique, Steven Spielberg took a piece of his heart, and transferred it, intact, onto a piece of celluloid. A simple and straightforward event, you would think, and yet an extremely rare and propitious occurrence. So even though our bell-bottom trousers and wide lapels look distinctly antiquated, the movie manages to feel as fresh and innovative today as it did in 1977. I'm proud to be part of it, and feel a bond, still, to everybody I was privileged to work with on it.

Truffaut passed away, sadly, seven years after the movie's release. The world lost a great artist and a wonderful man. He was only fifty-two, and yet he didn't waste a minute of the time he was given. He was well aware that even if he lived to be a hundred, he would never have enough time to film all the wonderful stories in his head. I often think about his decision only to make movies about the things that mattered most to him, and hope it offered him some consolation. He spent his last months quietly and with the dignity with which he lived his whole life.

I've never stopped thinking about the great similarity between Steven and François. On the surface, of course, both were tremendously different. One a suave French guy, the other an eager little kid from Arizona. And yet each was gifted with a similar ability to touch the heart. Spielberg wanted Truffaut for the movie from its very inception, and I wonder if he sensed, somehow, a kindred spirit.

Steven continually amazes us with the range and depth of his work. He grows, and constantly changes, yet manages never to lose his sense of wonder. He's also one of the rare Hollywood supernovas who burns as brightly at home with his family as he does on the set. Looking back on his career it's easy to see how deeply his connections to his wife, his children and his parents have informed every aspect of his work, and will probably continue to do so. I will always be first in line to buy a ticket for the next Spielberg attraction.

I keep in touch with Doug Trumbull, who created the special effects for

*Close Encounters*, as well as *2001* and many other classic movies. He continues to be a leader in his field, and is still hard at work revolutionizing the special effects industry. He's invented a system of cameras, cranes and a blue screen set-up that's convenient and portable. I went to his studio last month to watch as he put his recent creations into operation for a new television series, and the effects were amazing. He will remain in the vanguard of this extremely rigorous discipline, I trust, as long as he continues to feel like putting in his sixteen-hour days.

I look at the current generation of computer generated special effects in movies with some irony and a fair amount of nostalgia. I can't help but think that *CE3K* felt realer and less 'manufactured' than a lot of films we're watching today. When Steven finalized the effects sequences during those long and grueling months of post-production, he was literally inventing ways of combining live action with optical effects. He wrote the new vocabulary. The end product was revolutionary, and in some ways it has never been duplicated.

Today you can literally depict anything you want to, and spend as long as you like staring right into its mouth, if you wish. When Steven and Doug were putting together *Close Encounters*, the goal was different. How could you expose as *little* of a special effect as possible, and still get its point across? How could the story best be told, and a sense of believability be maintained? The ability to show everything, all the time, isn't necessarily an asset.

I'm reminded of the simple, nuts and bolts effect that allowed the objects in Neary's car to float mysteriously upwards, following Stanley Donen's example so ingeniously arrived at twenty-six years earlier, when he taught Fred Astaire to dance on the ceiling in *Royal Wedding*. Could either scene have been enhanced by our new technology? Sometimes 'in the camera' magic remains the best kind. It's easy to underestimate an audience's uncanny ability to sense the truth, whether it's in a performance, or the special effects, or the screenplay. You had to believe the effects in *CE3K* were real if you were to make that leap of faith and take the fantastic journey that Roy Neary did, and fortunately, Steven managed to enable all of us to do that.

I attended the twentieth anniversary of the movie at a special 'Academy' screening five years ago. It was the first time we had seen the newly restored print and heard its beautifully enhanced soundtrack. A packed house watched in rapt attention as the Mothership hovered over Devil's Tower, and the sound and light show cast its spell. I sat next to a lot of people who were still my close friends, and another who was a relative stranger, but whom I recognized instantly. Little Cary Guffey, now in his twenties, looked as if someone had taken his image from the movie and enlarged it. He was very much an adult, and at least six feet tall, but I don't think I've ever seen anyone grow up to look so much like themselves as a child. As a four year-old he was exceptionally calm, focused and cheerful. The current Guffey seems much the same.

I loved watching Guffey getting reacquainted with his movie mom, Melinda Dillon. He looked twenty years older. She looked exactly the same. It was easy to flash back to the tearful reunion of their characters in front of the Mothership, on the Big Set in Mobile, Alabama. They had a million things to say to each other. Grown up Cary and his wife Michelle live outside Birmingham, Alabama, not far from Melinda Dillon's family. The two families still exchange Christmas cards. The Guffeys are expecting their first child soon.

Cary works for Merrill Lynch as a financial advisor. After *CE3K* he continued to work as an actor for seven or eight years. After graduating from the University of Florida, he wrote Spielberg a letter telling him how confused he was about his future. Steven told Cary he should try on new hats, and not be worried. Steven was sure he would find his way. Cary tells me that he took Steven's advice, taught at a children's museum, had a great time, and then decided to go back to college to get his Master's degree in Finance.

He looks back on his experiences on *Close Encounters* fondly, and says that he was happy to learn at such an early age to be creative, and use his imagination. He remembers being carried around on the set, as the 'aliens' took him away, and recalls that Steven brought him to look around in advance so that he wouldn't be afraid. I asked him what he most remembered from the experience, and he says he never forgot the control panel on the set that made the kitchen go crazy during his friendly abduction. Having adults tell him that it was "OK to pretend" had a profound effect on his life. He tells me he is still "trying on different hats".

Melinda and I worked together several years after *CE3K* on the movie *Absence of Malice*, for which she was nominated for an Academy Award. My character was responsible for her character's suicide, and I hope she's forgiven me.

I've worked with Teri Garr a number of times. We've been married twice, filmically speaking, most recently in *Ghost World*. I'm taking her to the première of my new movie, *Gosford Park*, in Los Angeles this Friday night. I produced and acted in it, and am keeping all my fingers and toes crossed. Robert Altman has done a brilliant job directing it, and I was one extremely lucky, short character actor to have hooked up with the likes of him. We shot the movie in England last Spring, and it stars Maggie Smith, Emily Watson, Clive Owen, Helen Mirren, Kristin Scott Thomas, and almost every other British movie star you can think of. Teri has a beautiful seven year-old daughter, Molly, and is currently being funny and charming on *Hollywood Squares*.

During the last quarter century I've been broadening my horizons as much as I can. I'm producing, writing and directing, and I've been continuing to act in movies and on stage, on and off Broadway. I've been on TV a couple of times. I played the head of NBC on *Seinfeld* for five episodes. My character eventually fell madly in love with Elaine, not a hard thing to do, and ended up getting rejected, joined Greenpeace, and drowned at sea on a 'Save the Whales' expedition. If you added up all of my screen time on the show it would total about thirty minutes, and yet it's probably the most recognizable character in my vast repertoire of lawyers and scientists and executives. My character was called Russell Dalrymple, and was based on my friend Warren Littlefield, the real president of NBC at the time. A couple of years later I portrayed the actual Warren Littlefield, on a successful HBO movie called *The Late Shift*, based on the late night talk show wars.

I'm producing, directing and acting in a pilot for NBC with some of my pals from *Best in Show*, the Christopher Guest movie about crazy dog lovers. Our pilot's called *Adult Situations*, and we'll be doing it in the Spring. We were all in *Waiting for Guffman* a few years ago, and had a lot of fun working together. I think Truffaut would have liked that film. He was very fond of American comedies. I think about François a lot. When I go to a movie, I write my own review first, and then I think about how many thumbs up Truffaut would have given it.

I flash on a chilly Spring day in Massachusetts. It was three or four years ago, and I was traveling with my Dad. He died last month. He was an extremely youthful ninety-two, and we went on great vacations together. We talked about every topic imaginable, and never ran out of things to say. On one of our journeys we found ourselves at a spa called Canyon Ranch, where a mutual friend decided to introduce us to a woman she thought might hit it off with my Dad, who was ever on the lookout for new and interesting female companionship.

We all met in the lobby, and for fifteen minutes sparks flew as my father flirted and talked with an incredibly charming and attractive woman of around ninety. Her first husband, it turns out, was Truffaut's idol, Ernst Lubitsch, who happened to have been brought to Paramount by my uncle, Barney Balaban, who was president of the studio at the time. Lubitsch went on to make some of his classic romantic comedies for Paramount, like *One Hour With You* and *Trouble in Paradise*. They were charming, and light-footed, and erudite. Not unlike François.

All I could think about was what a kick Truffaut would have gotten out of the whole thing, and how sorry I was he was no longer around to hear my latest anecdote. Lubitsch's movies, and François' affection for them was a frequent topic under the hot lights of the Mothership. Truffaut felt Lubitsch was an enormous influence on his career — 'Close Encounters of the Six

Degrees of Separation Kind'.

Dreyfuss and I continue to be good friends. Last year we sat in the Carnegie Delicatessen, sharing a bowl of Matzoh Ball soup, and a waiter approached the table nervously and said, "Mr Dreyfuss, may I have your autograph?" As Richard located a pen and spread out a napkin on which to sign, the waiter pointed in my direction and said, I swear to God, "No, I meant him." I still have no idea why anyone would ever confuse us. Though no one has ever, to my knowledge, gotten us so mixed up that they sent me one of his paychecks.

Back in 1981, I acted with Richard in the film version of *Whose Life Is It Anyway?*, and next week I'm guest starring on his TV series *Max Bickford*, playing his best friend. We're looking forward to adjoining rooms in the old actors' home. He was kind enough to make a cameo appearance in a short film I made, called *SPFX 1140*, a comedy about a man who makes special effects. Bran Ferren, a special effects wizard whom I got to know during *2010*, let me film in his lab, and the short got me a job directing the pilot of *Tales From the Darkside*.

*Tales* was created by another genre guy, George Romero, who wrote and directed the terrifying movie *Night of the Living Dead*. The pilot starred Barnard Hughes, with whom I acted in my first movie, *Midnight Cowboy*. It's about a cruel miser who gets his frightening comeuppance on Hallowe'en, and ends up literally going to hell. The pilot spawned a series that ran for about a hundred and fifty episodes.

The pilot got me started on a directing career. One of my first TV episodic jobs was directing Spielberg's series *Amazing Stories*. Once again I was on a spaceship with Steven Spielberg. Only this time I was directing, he was producing, and the aliens on board were on their way to bring back Milton Berle instead of Richard Dreyfuss. Since then I've directed several movies and a number of TV shows.

One of the movies I directed, *Parents*, became something of an after mid-night cult hit. It was about a couple in 1958, who dress beautifully and spend a lot of time keeping up with the Joneses. They maintain a meticulous house and are excellent parents, except for the fact that they eat people. Randy Quaid and Mary Beth Hurt played Mom and Dad, and Sandy Dennis was their son's school psychologist, whom they kill and then devour at a big family meal at the end of the movie.

I saw the movie as a metaphor for my childhood. I grew up in the Midwest in the fifties, in a family that spent a fair amount of energy making sure that the rest of the world thought they were perfect, while keeping the family secrets under a tight lock and key. As it turns out, of course, my family's secrets weren't more horrific than those of any of the other families who lived in my peaceful little neighborhood, but I've always gotten nervous when I sensed people were hiding things. *Parents* tapped right into my childhood apprehensions.

I occasionally run into Julia Phillips, who's perhaps most famous now for writing a bestselling book about Hollywood called *You'll Never Eat Lunch in This Town Again*. As the producer of *Close Encounters* she was fiercely loyal to Steven, and tremendously supportive of the entire project. She kept those nervous executives at bay more than a few times, and I later developed a movie with her when she was an executive at Fox. [Sadly, she died of cancer in January 2002.] Susan Heldfond, who did such a great job teaching the extraterrestrials to wave their hands and do the alien dance, married Teddy Saunders, the brother of one of my best friends, Lanna Pressman. If we all live long enough, one of the little alien girls' kids will probably grow up to marry Cary Guffey's child. Alan Hynek's son can be Best Man.

I had another acting gig that actually took me into outer space. I played the wise and mysterious Dr Chandra, creator of the infamous computer, Hal, in the sequel to *2001*. Peter Hyams directed *2010*, and Roy Scheider starred. I was lucky enough to work with Helen Mirren, who co-starred as a Russian cosmonaut, and now stars, as Clive Owen's mother, in my current movie, *Gosford Park*. We compared notes on the challenges of special effects acting, and I talked about the many months I spent looking at nothing during *CE3K*. We spent about as long aboard our spaceship at MGM for *2010* as we spent in Mobile, Alabama and Gillette, Wyoming combined. If I spend many more days breathing the special effects fog that seems to fill every spaceship I've encountered, I'll have to send my lungs to the cleaners.

I spent several days alone, inside Hal the computer, shooting a critical scene. I was attached to a long steel rod, that was connected to a body cast I wore under my space-suit, and endured many hours being dangled upside down and sideways, like a chicken on a spit. At the end of the week I had a severe vertigo attack, and damaged my inner ear so badly I still experience occasional after-effects...

I recently created an animated series called *Very Lost in Space*, for Joe Roth's company. He used to run Disney, and now heads a production company called Revolution, along with Julia Roberts, and a few other talented folk. It can be seen on Sony's 'Screenblast' website. It's an improvised cartoon about a bunch of strange people on a spaceship. I play one of the strange people. The mission is so secret nobody will tell us where we're going, and nobody has taught us how to fly the ship. I decided to parody my character from *2010*, and we just finished a scene in which I upset Hal, the ever sensitive computer, and he starts to cry, threatening to rust the spaceship. This outer space thing has definitely become a recurrent theme in my life.

I explored inner space in *Altered States*, the Ken Russell movie that starred Bill Hurt. I worked with the makeup genius Dick Smith, whom I also encountered on *2010*. (Dick made my body cast for *2010*. He's worked on many classic movies over the years, and among many illustrious accomplishments, he created the original makeup for *The Exorcist*). I didn't get to fly in this one, but I watched as Bill Hurt revisited his molecular roots after taking hallucinogens and spending a few refreshing minutes in that quintessential sixties relaxation device, the sensory deprivation tank. Paddy Chayevsky, who wrote *Network* and *Marty* and a lot of other wonderful plays and films, wrote the movie, and I spent about seven months in Los Angeles shooting it. I never did get inside one of those tanks.

Dr Alan Hynek passed away a number of years ago. We maintained contact, and I loved reading his monthly newsletter. He published a rigorously researched report, in which he investigated UFO phenomena and gave detailed follow-ups on his findings. His tone was crisp and scientific, and, although he did uncover a number of events for which no rational or scientific explanations were possible, he steadfastly refused to call any of the sightings he investigated flying saucers, or jump to any conclusions as to the origin of what was being reported. An event was either able to be identified, or not. Off the record he was willing to venture a couple of guesses, including the theory of an 'alternate reality', but he was first and foremost a respected scientist, and would never have proposed a conclusion that he couldn't back up with a fact. I often think of Project Blue Book, his twenty-year project for the government, and the photographs of the unidentified saucer-shaped objects Alan himself took while flying on an airplane. I think one of the reasons *Close Encounters* continues to hold such fascination for people is that we are all desperate to believe there really *is* something out there, and that we are truly not alone.

A commonly held myth about the film is that Steven was somehow psychically compelled to tell the story to prepare us for an eventual visit from an actual spaceship. I must confess that I cannot imagine there is any truth to that urban legend, but wouldn't it be wonderful if it were true? How comforting to imagine that outer space is inhabited by imaginative and gentle creatures who want, more than anything, to introduce us peacefully to their world. I don't think the world has ever needed that particular fantasy more than we do at this exact moment in history.

I traveled to Poland and Budapest four years ago, to make a movie with Robin Williams called *Jakob the Liar*. It's a fictitious but realistically told story about Jews in a ghetto in Poland during World War II. I played a despairing barber, to whom Robin offers up a shred of good news by inventing reports received from a non-existent radio. Everywhere we went in Poland we heard stories about Steven and the filming of *Schindler's List*, which had been shot in the vicinity of some of our locations. His movie not only introduced a generation of people who had never heard of the Holocaust to its horrors, it managed to confound the cynics who never dreamed there would be an audience for such a movie. Steven followed up the film with discussion groups and lectures in schools around the world, and his Shoah Foundation continues to record and preserve testimony from Holocaust survivors and their families. The same kind and loving impulse to reach out that imbued the fantasy world of *CE3K* matured and grew into the harsh realities of *Schindler's List*.

## DECEMBER 12

I'm sitting in a hotel room in Los Angeles. It's four o'clock in the morning, and I can't sleep, so I'm attempting to finish this chapter, and come up with something insightful to say about *Close Encounters* for its twenty-fifth birthday. I'm mentally and physically exhausted. I've been attending pre-mières of *Gosford Park* in both New York and Los Angeles, and shuttling to Toronto to complete filming a cameo in a new Jackie Chan movie called *The Tuxedo*. I have just walked off an enormous set, depicting the lair of a mad scientist out to destroy the world. Jackie Chan is attempting to stop him, and I have a feeling he'll be successful. Once again, I breathed the required ten gallons of special effects smoke, and once again I worked for Steven Spielberg — his company, Dreamworks, is producing the film.

I worked for Steven's company last year, on a movie called *The Mexican*, in which Julia Roberts shot a hole in my neck. We filmed the sequence in a tiny village in Mexico, and I was in much greater danger from the food than I was from Julia. I also worked with Jim Carrey last year, in a film called *The Majestic*, directed by Frank Darabont. I'm looking forward to attending its star-studded and very glamorous opening tomorrow night at Hollywood's newly refurbished Egyptian Theatre. I have another one of my 'bad guy who does something evil in the first five minutes and then appears at the end to put the nail in the coffin' roles, and I can't wait to see it. I think Jim will be terrific, and I love Frank's work.

In my few moments of spare time I'm finishing writing a book for Scholastic, the publisher that brought us *Harry Potter* in the US. It will bring us *McGrowl*, in the Fall, if I can complete it by Christmas. It looks like I'll get there. It's the story of a boy and his adventures with his bionic dog. I'm having a lot of fun, and it's something I've never done before. The most grandiose of my fantasies is, of course, a Steven Spielberg production of the movie version, in yet another twist on a 'Close Encounter'. But who wouldn't dream about that.

---

When I was a little boy I used to go into my backyard and stare up at the sky, and try to focus on one particular star. I would concentrate with all my might, and beam a thought up at it. I knew the star was billions of light years away, but I didn't care. I told the star that I was on a planet revolving around a different star, and that if there was anybody out there listening — and I didn't care if they replied — they should at least know there was somebody else out there, and they were looking at them. I liked to think that maybe a person, or a thing, or a creature, was up there looking back at me, and thinking a similar thought. And maybe, I thought, given the limitless number of stars and planets that whirled around up there, maybe this event was actually occurring and I wasn't losing my mind. It's not impossible for me to imagine that Spielberg was out there in his backyard, thinking the same weird thoughts. I know that this kind of thinking isn't going to get you anywhere (except possibly into an institution), but it's fun to dream.

We need to know that we are not alone. We catch glimpses of ourselves, from time to time, sitting on our miniscule planet, in our unimportant little solar system, whirling around our relatively insignificant sun in a void in the middle of a black hole, surrounded by decaying stars and exploding galaxies. We cannot think that we are the only ones out here, because it is far too terrifying and much too lonely. Somehow Steven knew this and he gave us *Close Encounters*. He made us a little bit less afraid, and gave us a ray of hope to cling to.

Who knows what the next twenty-five years has in store for us? The events of last Fall have reminded us never to take anything for granted. I'll certainly do my best to stay busy, and keep the wolf away from my door. I hope I get to make more movies, and breathe some more special effects smoke, and maybe write some more books. Hopefully, I'll get to be a grandfather, and hopefully one of my grandchildren will enjoy watching *Close Encounters*, as much as I enjoyed being a little part of it. Maybe he or she will read this book, and know that even before they were born I was sitting around thinking about them. And maybe Michael Rennie really will arrive, finally, in his gleaming flying saucer and warn us all to get along together and stop fighting or the Earth will go away forever, the way he did in *The Day the Earth Stood Still*. And maybe, as Jiminy Cricket tells us at the end of *Close Encounters of the Third Kind*, if we keep wishing on a star our dreams really will come true. So far it seems to be working for me.

# THE CAST AND CREW

Roy Neary ................................................RICHARD DREYFUSS
Claude Lacombe ............................................FRANCOIS TRUFFAUT
Ronnie Neary ...................................................................TERI GARR
Jillian Guiler ........................................................MELINDA DILLON
David Laughlin.........................................................BOB BALABAN
Robert.............................................................LANCE HENRIKSEN
Wild Bill ........................................................WARREN KEMMERLING
Farmer.............................................................ROBERTS BLOSSOM
Jean Claude............................................................PHILLIP DODDS
Barry Guiler............................................................CARY GUFFEY
Brad Neary................................................................SHAWN BISHOP
Sylvia Neary................................................ADRIENNE CAMPBELL
Toby Neary ..........................................................JUSTIN DREYFUSS
Team Leader ....................................................MERRILL CONNALLY
Major Benchley...................................................GEORGE DICENZO

Produced by...........................................JULIA PHILLIPS and MICHAEL PHILLIPS
Written & Directed by...........................................STEVEN SPIELBERG
Director of Photography ..........................................VILMOS ZSIGMOND, A.S.C.
Special Photographic Effects by.......................................DOUGLAS TRUMBULL
Music by ...............................................................JOHN WILLIAMS
Director of Photography, Additional American Scenes

                                                WILLIAM A. FRAKER, A.S.C.

Director of Photography, Special Sequences, India

                                                DOUGLAS SLOCOMBE, B.S.C.

# THE CAST AND CREW

Production Designer............................................................................JOE ALVES
Edited by........................................................................MICHAEL KAHN, A.C.E.
Associate Producer.......................................................................CLARK PAYLOW
Visual Effect Concepts by..............................................STEVEN SPIELBERG
Unit Production Manager...........................................................CLARK PAYLOW
Additional Directors of Photography............................JOHN ALONZO, A.S.C.,
LASZLO KOVACS, A.S.C.
Technical Advisor..............................................................DR. J. ALLEN HYNEK
Art Director ...............................................................................DAN LOMINO
Set Decoration........................................................................PHIL ABRAMSON
Assistant Director.......................................................................CHUCK MYERS
2nd Assistant Director ..................................................................JIM BLOOM
Assistant Film Editors ...................GEOFF ROWLANDS, CHARLES BORNSTEIN
Music Editor ...............................................................KENNETH WANNBERG
Supervising Sound Effects Editor ...........................................FRANK WARNER
Sound Effects Editorial Staff...................RICHARD OSWALD, DAVID HORTEN,
SAM GEMETTE, GARY S. GERLICH,
CHET SLOMKA, NEIL BURROW
Production Illustrator ...............................................................GEORGE JENSEN
Dolby Sound Supervisor .................................................................STEVE KATZ
Supervising Dialogue Editor ...................................................JACK SCHRADER
Dialogue Editorial Staff...............................................................DICK FRIEDMAN
Production Sound Mixer ...........................................................GENE CANTAMESA
Music Scoring Mixer ........................................................................JOHN NEAL
Mothership, Tuba Solo.............................................................TOMMY JOHNSON
Light Board, Oboe Solo .................................................................JOHN ELLIS
Camera Operator .........................................................................NICK McLEAN
Re-recording Mixers.........BUZZ KNUDSE, DON MacDOUGAL, ROBERT GLASS
Location Manager .......................................................................JOE O'HAR
Gaffer ......................................................................................EARL GILBERT
Assistant to the Producer.....................................................KENDALL COOPER
Director's Assistant......................................................................RICK FIELDS
Production Secretary....................................................................GAIL SIEMERS
Production Staff ...........................SALLY DENNISO, JANET HEALE, PAT BURNS
A.F.I. Intern.............................................................................SETH WINSTON
Makeup Supervisor...........................................................BOB WESTMORELAND
Hairdresser .................................................................................EDIE PANDA
Property Master .......................................................................SAM GORDON
Wardrobe Supervisor....................................................................JIM LINN
Stunt Coordinator...........................................................BUDDY JOE HOOKER
Script Supervision...................................................................CHARLSIE BRYANT

Casting ...........................................................SHARI RHODES, JULIETTE TAYLOR
Additional Casting ...............................................SALLY DENNISON
Publicity ...................................................MARVIN LEVY, MURRAY WEISSMAN,
AL EBNER, PICKWICK PUBLIC RELATIONS
Still Photographers...............................PETER SOREL, JIM COE, PETE TURNER
Title Designer...................................................................DAN PERRI
2nd Unit Director of Photography...............................................STEVE POSTER
Location Auditor.......................................................STEVE WARNER
Construction Manager ...............................................BILL PARKS
Special Effects Consultant .....................................ROY ARBOGAST
Assistant to François Truffaut...........................................FRANCOISE FORGET
Special Photographic Effects Supervised By...................DOUGLAS TRUMBULL
Director of Photography, Photographic Effects ...............RICHARD YURICICH
Matte Artist..........................................................MATTHEW YURICICH
Special Effects Editor .............................................LARRY ROBINSON
UFO Photography .......................................................DAVE STEWART
Effects Unit Project Manager...............................ROBERT SHEPHERD
Chief Model Maker....................................................GREGORY JEIN
Animation Supervision ......................................ROBERT SWARTHE
Matte Camera Operator..................................................DON JAREL
Project Coordinator........................................MONA THAL BENEFIEL
Camera Operators...........................................ROBERT HALL, EUGENE EYERLY,
DENNIS MUREN, ELDON RICKMAN
Technician .............................................................ROBERT HOLLISTER
Assistant Cameramen.........................DAVID HARDBERGER, ALAN HARDING,
BILL MILLAR, MAXWELL MORGAN,
RICHARD RIPPEL, SCOTT SQUIARES
Still Photography..........................................................MARCIA REID
Model Shop Coordinator........................................J. RICHARD DOW
Model Makers...............................................PAUL HUSTON, DAVID M. JONES,
JOR VAN KLINE, MICHAEL McMILLEN,
KENNETH SWENSON, ROBERT WORTHINGTON
Camera and Mechanical Design..........DON TRUMBULL (B.G. ENGINEERING)
JOHN RUSSELL, FRIES ENGINEERING
Mechanical Special Effects .........................................GEORGE POLKINGHORNE
Electronics Design ...................................JERRY L. JEFFRESS, ALVAH J. MILLER,
PETER REGLA, DAN SLATER
Assistant Matte Artist ................................................ROCCO GIOFFRE
Effects Electrician .......................................................DAVID GOLD
Key Grip.....................................................................RAY RICH
Laboratory Expeditor ...............................................CHARLES HINKLE

## THE CAST AND CREW

Animator ..................................................................................HARRY MOREAU
Animation Staff..............................CAROL BOARDMAN, ELEANOR DAHLAN,
CY DIDJURGIS, TOM KOESTER, CONNE MORGAN
Production Secretary..............................................................JOYCE GOLDBERG
Production Accountant..............................................................PEGGY ROSSON
Project Assistants....................................GLENN ERICKSON, HOYT YATEMAN
Editorial Assistant..................................................................JOSEPH IPPOLITO
Transportation .........................................................................BILL BETHEA
Laboratory Technicians .....................................DON DOW, TOM HOLLISTER
Negative Cutter................................................................BARBARA MORRISON
Special Consultants .............................PETER ANDERSON, LARRY ALBRIGHT,
RICHARD BENNETT, KEN EBERT,
KEVIN KELLY, JIM LUTES, GEORGE RANDALL,
JEFF SHAPIRO, ROURKE ENGINEERING